The Ethics of Entrepreneurship Education

The Ethics of
Entrepreneurship Education

Kyle Jensen

The MIT Press

Cambridge, Massachusetts | London, England

The MIT Press would like to thank the anonymous peer reviewers who provided comments on drafts of this book. The generous work of academic experts is essential for establishing the authority and quality of our publications. We acknowledge with gratitude the contributions of these otherwise uncredited readers.

This book was set in Stone Serif and Stone Sans by Westchester Publishing Services. Printed and bound in the United States of America.

Library of Congress Cataloging-in-Publication Data

Names: Jensen, Kyle, 1977– author.
Title: The ethics of entrepreneurship education / Kyle Jensen.
Description: Cambridge, Massachusetts : The MIT Press, 2024. | Includes
    bibliographical references and index.
Identifiers: LCCN 2023050136 (print) | LCCN 2023050137 (ebook) |
    ISBN 9780262549479 (paperback) | ISBN 9780262380461 (epub) |
    ISBN 9780262380478 (pdf)
Subjects: LCSH: Entrepreneurship—Study and teaching (Higher)—United
    States. | Education, Higher—Moral and ethical aspects—United States.
Classification: LCC HB615 .J464 2024 (print) | LCC HB615 (ebook) |
    DDC 174/.4—dc23/eng/20231204
LC record available at https://lccn.loc.gov/2023050136
LC ebook record available at https://lccn.loc.gov/2023050137

10 9 8 7 6 5 4 3 2 1

Contents

Preface

I wrote this book to help readers identify and think through common ethical problems that arise in entrepreneurship education. But more than that, I wrote this book for myself. It is both a narrative and formalization of my quest to understand what I "ought to do" when I encounter ethical problems teaching entrepreneurship.

While my primary audience is faculty and staff in higher education who instruct student entrepreneurs, I hope this book will also be useful to the broad assemblage of stakeholders who participate in university entrepreneurship ecosystems: mentors, investors, alumni, service providers, and of course, student entrepreneurs themselves. I have played many of those roles myself and tried to bring the perspective from each into the book.

At this writing, I am an associate dean at the Yale School of Management, a senior lecturer, and the Shanna and Eric Bass '05 Director of Entrepreneurial Programs. In that capacity, I coordinate a small phalanx of fantastic faculty who teach courses in entrepreneurship, and oversee a variety of extracurricular programs, including fellowships and speaker series. I teach entrepreneurship classes, particularly those related to tech entrepreneurship, and work with dozens of campus entrepreneurs outside the classroom at any given time.

Prior to teaching, I was a volunteer mentor and entrepreneur-in-residence at Yale. Before that, I cofounded three ventures: two software companies, Rho AI and PriorSmart; and Agrivida, a biotech company I cofounded as a graduate student at the Massachusetts Institute of Technology.

By most metrics, I was a successful entrepreneur, although by no means the kind to grace the cover of magazines or garner similar accolades. All three of my ventures were acquired; a couple even made me a decent amount of money. Between these ventures, I also worked for a nonprofit organization called PIPRA (the Public Intellectual Property Resource for Agriculture), helping universities in developing economies to establish technology licensing offices and other programs in support of faculty entrepreneurship.

While this book discusses many ethical problems, none have the severity of the typical fare found in applied ethics books; there are no life-and-death situations. The famous trolley problem never shows up.[1] The problems discussed in this book are trifling by contrast, but what they lack in severity, they make up for in frequency. They arise often in entrepreneurship education, and I am convinced that their examination makes for better educators.

I suspect most entrepreneurship educators—coming from business, engineering, and science backgrounds—have spent far more time with calculators and computers than with the classics of normative ethics, even if they got some exposure in survey courses as undergraduates. So I made an effort herein to describe the major theories of normative ethics and connect these to the problems faced by entrepreneurship educators. I also did my best not to dither but instead to recommend courses of action in an effort to make this book a *practical* resource. I'm certain some readers will disagree with my conclusions and opinions—which is fine. As Scottish philosopher David Hume wrote,

> Reasonable [persons] may be allowed to differ where no one can
> reasonably be positive: Opposite sentiments, even without any

decision, afford an agreeable amusement; and if the subject be curious and interesting, the book carries us, in a manner, into company, and unites the two greatest and purest pleasures of human life: study and society.[2]

If you disagree with my conclusions here, I hope you at least find the subject "curious and interesting."

Acknowledgments

I am obliged most of all to Scott Cooper. I sought an editor for this book; in Scott I found both an editor and friend. I am also indebted to Bill Aulet, Tristan Botelho, Tom Byers, Jonas Clark, Laura Dunham, Jon Fjeld, Matthew Grimes, Song Ma, Jennifer McFadden, Kathryn Miller-Jensen, Fiona Murray, Barry Nalebuff, Heidi Neck, Patricia Resio, Olav Sorenson, Siri Terjesen, Robert Wuebker, Ted Zoller, and the great students and alumni of Yale University.

1
An Ethical Dilemma

On an autumn day early in my career at Yale, I went for a walk around campus with Peter, a wealthy donor to the university. Meeting with donors is one of the best parts of my job; they're usually fascinating, successful people who care about Yale and its good work in the world. Like many donors, Peter had himself been an entrepreneur—that's how he came into his wealth—although in recent years he had become a well-known investor. The fall foliage and Yale's neo-Gothic architecture made a pleasant backdrop for a pleasant conversation.

As we returned to my office at the School of Management, Peter said, "Jill Brown came to see me about investing in her start-up. Do you know her? What do you think of her?"

I knew Jill well and thought highly of her. She and I worked closely together, meeting weekly as a condition of her enrollment in our "practicum"—a class in which student entrepreneurs work on their ventures *for credit*, with the aim of bringing their Yale education to bear on the advancement of their entrepreneurial endeavors. Because of our faculty-student relationship and our work in the practicum, I knew a great deal about Jill's venture. I had seen her "pitch"—the presentation entrepreneurs give describing their start-ups—and it was persuasive. But I suspected Peter was unaware of something I knew: Jill's persuasive pitch omitted some *substantial* caveats. Her start-up was not as great as it seemed at first glance.

That was one of the first moments in which I recall myself marveling at the ethical complexity of entrepreneurship education. I was unsure what to tell this donor. On the one hand, I thought I should speak highly of Jill. She was my student, after all, and I want my students to find investors. On the other hand, I feared this donor's investment in Jill would go sour and lead to a variety of unattractive outcomes, particularly him distrusting my judgment in the future, not investing in my other students, and being disinclined to donate to Yale in support of my programs. Did I have an obligation to keep Jill's information confidential? What I knew of her venture came exclusively from our private conversations *in a class* in which I was her instructor. We spoke about her conflicts with her cofounders, indecision about pursuing the venture, struggles to hold her team together, and the threat of competitors. Surely such details were offered in confidence. I could betray this confidence without uttering a word; a shrug or wink would be enough to ward off the investor based on what I knew. I wanted to ingratiate myself with this donor and keep this donor-investor happy, but I feared betraying the trust Jill had placed in me.

I fumbled for an answer to Peter's question about Jill, unsure of what was "right," best, or ethical. I had, I realize now, stumbled headlong onto one of the numerous ethical land mines that litter the terrain of entrepreneurship education at Yale—indeed, at every college or university where entrepreneurship is taught. (From now on, I use the word "university" to refer to both colleges and universities, as they are understood in the United States.)

*   *   *

This is a book about those ethical land mines, like the one I faced with Jill—the numerous predicaments that university educators grapple with when teaching entrepreneurship. For example, should faculty keep information about student start-ups confidential? Should educators personally invest in student start-ups? Should the university? Should educators or representatives of the university serve on company boards? Should educators adjudicate disputes between founders, such as by dictating how stock is split between students who create a start-up in class? Should the university and its educators play "matchmaker" between student founders, investors, attorneys, and other service providers?

As an entrepreneurship educator, I struggle daily with these questions. Campus entrepreneurship brings *profit* in conflict with *pedagogy*. In this way, it is like other potentially lucrative endeavors on campus such as college sports and university-administered hospital systems: that which is best for the education of a student entrepreneur, athlete, or medical resident can often be at odds with what benefits the university.[1] Students involved in these activities can be easily, and even unwittingly, exploited by the university and its educators.

Thanks to the fantastic success and proliferation of entrepreneurship education, this topic is more relevant than ever. In the United States, universities are now wellsprings of entrepreneurship. We produce prodigious numbers of both young entrepreneurs and the innovations that become start-ups.

This did not happen by chance but rather through sustained investment by governments and universities in policies and programs supporting entrepreneurship. US universities embraced the Bayh-Dole Act, which bequeathed to them ownership of the formal intellectual property (IP) arising from federally funded research and led to an explosion in tech-based start-up companies on campus.[2] At the same time, universities dramatically expanded educational opportunities in entrepreneurship.[3] In 1985, there were 250 courses in entrepreneurship offered at US universities; by 2010, that number had grown to roughly 5,000, taught by 9,000 faculty serving some 400,000 students annually across thousands of universities.[4]

These courses are found in a broad assortment of university programs: bachelor's degrees, master's degrees, PhDs, minors, certificates, and nondegree concentrations.[5] Simultaneously, universities expanded their extracurricular support for campus entrepreneurs by building innovation spaces, creating start-up incubators/accelerators, and in some cases, investing in start-ups through university-sponsored venture capital funds.[6]

In short, US universities are different institutions than they were a generation ago; they are now suffused with start-up activity. And that's a good thing. Entrepreneurship evokes enthusiasm across campuses in ways that few other topics do. It is something behind which diverse departments rally—not only engineering and the sciences, areas with obvious interests in entrepreneurship, but the arts and humanities, for which the goals of social entrepreneurship resonate.

The boom in university entrepreneurship is great for society too. Empirical research shows that entrepreneurship produces job growth, regional economic development, aggregate wealth creation, and knowledge spillovers.[7] These benefits, however, are not produced in equal amounts by each entrepreneur; most come from those few entrepreneurs who create new, successful, high-growth start-ups— the Googles, Alibabas, and Genentechs. These sorts of ventures do not just change our world for the better but also make their founders into *billionaires*. Of course, financial outcomes like that are exceedingly unusual. The *median* entrepreneur creates *zero* net jobs and would be financially better off holding an S&P 500 index fund than their company's own stock.[8] (This is true whether you consider just entrepreneurs starting incorporated ventures or include sole proprietors, who are more numerous.)

There are, though, plenty of nonpecuniary rewards of entrepreneurship, including independence in the form of being your own boss; the flexibility to choose your own hours and work content; and self-exploration, testing your mettle through a challenge.[9] These benefits are distributed in a more egalitarian manner than the financial returns of entrepreneurship; even those who fail to become billionaires—or don't aspire to such wealth—can also enjoy them.

Joseph Schumpeter, one of the first economists to study entrepreneurs, described the motivations of entrepreneurs poetically:

> There is the will to conquer: the impulse to fight, to prove oneself superior to others, to succeed for the sake, not of the fruits of success, but of success itself. . . . [T]here is the joy of creating, of getting things done, or simply of exercising one's energy and ingenuity.[10]

These motivations are often invoked to explain the entrepreneur's choice of such a daunting vocation.[11] Most entrepreneurs work harder and bear more risk than their salaried compatriots. Few find "success." But in the aggregate, they perform an important and beneficial function in society as the architects of Schumpeter's famous "creative destruction," as the innovators who unseat incumbents and reallocate resources, forever renewing economies. For Schumpeter, they are the quintessential economic actor; views of the economy that ignore the entrepreneur are "like *Hamlet* without the Danish prince."[12]

The centrality of entrepreneurs in our capitalist system explains the attention they receive from policymakers, their exaltation in the press, and the enthusiasm for entrepreneurship at universities. Entrepreneurship *is* important, and universities are uniquely able to foster it.[13] No other institution has such a mix of cutting-edge technology and bright young souls willing to embark on risky world-changing endeavors.

The problem for universities, though, is that supporting these endeavors presents many ethical dilemmas.

Why Ethical Problems Arise in Entrepreneurship Education

There are many individual characteristics of entrepreneurship education in the university that make it wonderful and special.

Collectively, however, these same characteristics create substantial ethical problems that simply do not arise in mathematics, English, the basic sciences, or most other areas of study.

Let me spell out four of these individual characteristics and explore how problems arise.

- Many students studying entrepreneurship are not studying with the intention of merely becoming entrepreneurs later, after graduation. Instead, students are frequently entrepreneurs *during* their university studies.[14]

Philosopher Søren Kierkegaard wrote, "The highest and most beautiful things in life are not to be heard about, nor read about, nor seen but, if one will, are to be lived."[15] How magical that university students can not only *learn* about entrepreneurship on campus but also *live* it! This distinguishes entrepreneurship from other areas of study. Students heading to Wall Street are rarely financiers while at a university. Those studying civil engineering are not building bridges in town. Students who wish to go into consulting are not often paid, practicing consultants while in school. Sure, such students might do internships, but this is quite different from the student entrepreneur. Interns play a tune written by others; student founders write their own scores and simultaneously conduct the orchestra.

If no students chose to start ventures during their studies, entrepreneurship education would present fewer ethical dilemmas. We wouldn't have to worry about dividing the profits of ventures, keeping student venture information confidential, or adjudicating disputes between student cofounders. At the same time, though, the university would be a diminished place.

- Student entrepreneurs forge numerous business relationships on and off campus.

Entrepreneurship is a team sport that generally requires the contributions of many.[16] Student entrepreneurs who launch start-ups forge relationships with faculty, university staff administering entrepreneurship-related programs, mentors participating in those programs, cofounders both inside and outside the university, alumni, employees, investors, attorneys, accountants, other service providers, and of course customers (of which one hopes there will be large numbers).

These relationships are a *good thing*. Indeed, universities go out of their way to facilitate interactions between these parties; our student founders *need* to find investors, employees, customers, and so on. As Steve Blank, a thirty-year veteran of Silicon Valley tech start-ups, famously said, entrepreneurs need to "get out of the building." This exhortation applies less to students studying other subjects. It matters little to the physics student or classicist whether they get out of the building. In contrast, student entrepreneurs cannot succeed if they are sequestered in the library. Only with the aid of others can they build their ventures.

Yet forging so many relationships introduces the potential for ethical problems, if for no other reason than it creates more opportunity for ethical transgression. Entrepreneurs have higher ethical "surface area" than most other students. Which other students on campus create so many high-stakes relationships formalized through contracts, such as nondisclosure agreements (NDAs), engagement agreements, and debt or equity instruments? Again, these relationships are a *good thing*, but in all cases they introduce an ethical dimension in which persons must consider their rights and duties as parties to the relationship.

- Entrepreneurship education creates the potential for great wealth.

The potential for wealth creation is a stark distinction between entrepreneurship education and other subjects on campus. If students write a paper together in an English class, that paper rarely has even the slightest impact on their financial lives; it is relevant for the semester and probably forgotten thereafter. In contrast, a start-up idea conceived in class or a school-sponsored hackathon could be worth billions of dollars, although the odds of that are long. That value will accrue to the student entrepreneurs and potentially each of the stakeholders that participated in baking a proverbial "pie" together—cofounders, employees, investors, the university, and so on. Each may desire, many can expect, and some will deserve a piece of that pie.

So what's the ethical problem? It is that stakeholders may fight over this wealth, and in that battle, the university and its faculty risk abusing their power over young students.

- Entrepreneurship educators are often not just faculty but also investors, board members, advisers, and entrepreneurs themselves.

Entrepreneurship education puts a premium on *practice*, and *practitioners* are relatively common participants in the university entrepreneurship ecosystem.[17] In this regard, entrepreneurship is similar to disciplines like architecture and the arts. For example, faculty teaching entrepreneurship are often themselves also entrepreneurs or investors with substantial ties to the local community.[18] Put differently, entrepreneurship educators have complex "role-sets"—"complement[s] of role-relationships in which persons are involved by virtue of occupying a particular social status."[19] Ethical problems arise because these role-relationships have conflicting ethical norms.

The entrepreneur-investor relationship is transactional: the parties, as consenting adults, make some agreement in a competitive marketplace. In contrast, the educator-student relationship is not transactional but more akin to the relationships between attorneys or physicians and their client and patients—relationships characterized by high expertise asymmetry and trust placed in the professional.[20] These are the kinds of relationships in which the professional acquires a *fiduciary-like* responsibility to the client—a responsibility to act in a manner consistent with the client's best interests.

For educators, it can be unclear which ethical norms apply in which situations. For example, when a student entrepreneur meets with a faculty member to solicit investment in a start-up, are they in a student-faculty relationship or an entrepreneur-investor one? Does it matter whether the student is *currently* in a class with that faculty member or is in the faculty member's department? When a faculty adviser and graduate student launch a venture together, which relationship dominates: adviser-advisee or cofounders? When a faculty person advises a student on a patent license, whose interests is the faculty person serving? Those of the student? The start-up? The university? The faculty person's own?

You might ask if Yale and other schools have policies governing these situations, and why faculty can't simply defer to those. I have three responses.

First, whatever policies a university or college may have almost certainly suffer from "incomplete contracting" (see chapter 4). No policy can preclude all the myriad possible problems.

Second, most faculty are at best dimly aware of their university policies (aside from the policy on triennial leave). Anecdotal evidence suggests that faculty speed-click through their online workplace harassment training while watching Netflix.

Third, the efficacy of such policies is suspect. In many institutions, research productivity and tenure are a license to do what one pleases.

Having impugned the utility of policies, let me walk back my argument a bit. Policies are surely not harmful, but neither are they a panacea. This could be a book about what our policies should be. But better than that, it is more so a book about what is right and wrong, and how entrepreneurship educators should behave when our policies fail us, as they inevitably will. It is a book about how to make decisions and which priorities to put first.

In Homer's *The Odyssey*, Telemachus says, "If you serve too many masters, you'll soon suffer."[21] Educators teaching entrepreneurship or those otherwise involved in start-ups are often in dynamic situations where it is unclear who they are serving and what ethical norms apply at which moments. The risk for entrepreneurship educators is that we will bring the ethical norms of one domain into another and be derelict in our duties, particularly in our duties to students—that we will serve too many masters and thereby cause suffering, particularly for students.

*   *   *

These foregoing factors contribute to the ethical complexity of entrepreneurship education and resurface throughout the book. Each of the chapters that follow considers a class of ethical conundrums. I discuss the investment and involvement of universities and faculty with student start-ups; the relationship between student entrepreneurs and service providers such as venture capitalists and lawyers; how to grade entrepreneurship classes; and other topics. My aspiration, like that of Kierkegaard, is "to make difficulties everywhere," to raise your awareness of entrepreneurship education's ethical dimensions, and provide you, the reader, with practical advice for navigating the same.[22]

The book is also intensely personal. It is the product of my struggle to understand my experiences as a student entrepreneur and inventor, and then after school, as a mentor, investor, entrepreneurship educator, and university administrator. Stories from these roles pack this book's pages and motivate the chapters. They are stories that will be familiar to those of you who, like me, have the good fortune to be part of this most magical activity of modern universities.

2
University Investment and Involvement in Student Start-ups

I met Emma in my first year of teaching at Yale. She was an MBA candidate and founder of a start-up making software for restaurants that helped diners browse and order delicious dishes from their mobile devices before being seated. New Haven, Connecticut, has a thriving food scene, and Emma developed substantial traction in a short time. She spoke to customers continually. Emma signed deals before her products were built. She taught herself to code (albeit badly) and wasn't ashamed to ship a flawed alpha of her app.

I have fond memories of Emma standing on her desk in the middle of our entrepreneurship center, belting out her pitch in an effort to banish the jitters. She was the kind of entrepreneur with whom faculty love working.

As the school year ended, everyone was being pulled in different directions. Internship offers, significant others, and the manifold opportunities unfurling before bright students at the dawn of their professional careers were a challenge as Emma worked hard to hold her team together. It was in this context that she learned of her admission to one of our university's summer accelerator programs. It was a pretty typical intense, short-term, cohort-based program that provided a stipend of about $15,000, mentorship, and a rotating cast of experienced guest entrepreneurs who visited to share their wisdom.

To Emma, it was a godsend—just what she needed to keep her team from scattering into the wind over the summer. The summer accelerator also gave the impression that her start-up had Yale's blessing, which was something she could use to impress would-be investors.

I had known many students who participated in this accelerator in the past, and with rare exception, I knew they had a good experience. I was surprised when Emma asked me, "Would you take a look at this contract for the accelerator?" I obliged, curious because I was unfamiliar with any of those other students having had contractual obligations.

I discovered things were different that year. Students in the accelerator were being required to give Yale a participation right in their ventures, meaning that the university was granted a right, but not an obligation, to invest in the students' start-ups. The participation rights allowed the university to acquire up to 6 percent of the start-ups. Such rights are useful because they allow investors to wait and see. If a start-up is the next Facebook, investors can exercise their rights to buy the start-up's stock; if a start-up is a dud, investors can let the rights expire without putting up any money.

Yale was also requiring these students to pay the university 3 percent of the net proceeds if they sold their companies before raising venture capital. There were other new terms too. And some of the rights assigned to Yale were even fungible, meaning the university could sell or assign the rights to whomever it wished. Moreover, some obligations followed a student even if the venture went belly-up: if any of the student participants founded a similar venture in the following two years, Yale would have rights to the *new* venture.

These terms made me uneasy, so I forwarded the contract to a few professional investors and asked for their take. "I'm really appalled," said one. "Batshit," replied another.

I told Emma how I felt about the terms and suggested she push back. She returned to the accelerator, complaints in hand and ready to negotiate—but she was rebuffed. My colleagues running the accelerator told Emma that the terms were normal and "nonnegotiable."

What were my colleagues across campus thinking? I wondered. We are a university, not a venture capital firm. When we give a fellowship to budding thespians, artists, and authors, we don't ask for a portion of *their* future income. By what logic would we treat student entrepreneurs differently? Shouldn't we support student entrepreneurs the way we support other students around campus: modestly and without laying claim to their future wealth?

I also wondered whether I had been naive for not demanding a piece of the upside from the masses of entrepreneurs that *I* was mentoring at Yale. Maybe *I* should be getting participation rights that I could sell off?

Good Intentions

I knew these colleagues who were running the accelerator. They were well-intentioned, smart, and experienced. Furthermore, some among them could rightly claim to have done more for Yale entrepreneurs than anyone else at our university, including me. But I had to ask them to explain these new demands they were imposing on student entrepreneurs.

They had three rationales. First, they characterized the new contract as ensuring that successful students would "pay it forward." Many student start-ups would not exist were it not for Yale, went the argument. The university is the convener and cultivator of great people and ideas. Shouldn't student entrepreneurs who benefit from our environment contribute to its maintenance so that future generations may benefit similarly?

Second, the new contract was required, they claimed, because our administration wanted entrepreneurship programs to be financially self-sustaining. How would that happen if not through the profits of companies passing through the accelerator? To that they added that if the returns were good, our university's support for student entrepreneurs could be expanded, thereby helping *more* student start-ups and helping each student start-up *more*. All it would take is one Facebook-size return and the university would never again be short of funds to support student founders.

Third, they told me that other universities had similar contracts.

Each of these was a reasonable and understandable rationale. I was then, and I am now, sympathetic to their arguments. But I felt they were overlooking the perils created when universities act like venture capitalists—perils that trump whatever benefits the university might reap.

Twelfth-century French monk Bernard de Clairvaux is credited with the aphorism "L'enfer est plein de bonnes volontés ou désirs."[1] It means "hell is full of good wishes or desires"; our colloquial version is "the road to hell is paved with good intentions." Even with the best of intentions, universities investing in their students' companies can pave the way to . . . well, not hell, but at least significant perils for those institutions, both ethical and practical. That suggests strongly that such investing is a road best avoided.

Conflicts of Interest

Investing is an exchange: an investor gives an entrepreneur resources—typically money but potentially other resources—and in return the entrepreneur gives the investor an interest in the start-up, typically in the form of stock, warrants, participation rights, liquidity payments, or similar securities. When a university invests in its students' start-ups, the interest it receives creates a *conflict of interest* for the university and its educators.

Conflicts of interest are common enough in life, and they're not always unethical. For example, a judge who is related to a plaintiff in a lawsuit would have a conflict of interest and could manage that conflict by disclosing their relationship and recusing themselves from a case, which is completely ethical. A university is in a trickier position than this hypothetical judge because of the particular ethical duties that we, as educators, have toward students.

In part, "ethics" describes how we ought to comport ourselves in our relationships with others, and why some ways of treating others are right and different ways are wrong. But not all relationships are equal. Some are special relationships in which one party depends on and places great trust in another party. The "right and wrong" of such relationships are described by the field of *professional ethics*. In particular, professional ethics delineates the ethical obligations of persons in the small number of *professions* wherein self-regulating experts with specialized knowledge deliver vital services to their clients.[2] Think lawyers, doctors, clergy, professors, and a few others, but not hairdressers, car mechanics, or delivery persons.

In each of these professions, clients—broadly defined—trust a professional to make decisions in the clients' best interests. These are *fiduciary* relationships—such as between doctors and patients or professors and students.

Professional ethics, as typically understood, extends beyond mere ethical behavior or *business ethics* to describe the extra ethical obligations of professionals that they acquire in light of the trust bestowed on them by clients in these unequal relationships. These extra obligations usually include truth telling, confidentiality, and a duty to be the client's fiduciary: to pursue that which is in the client's best interest and prevent conflicts of interest.[3] Further, each profession has distinct ethical obligations related to the specific services provided to its clients. For example, the American Medical Association maintains a code of medical ethics, and the American Bar Association maintains a similar "Models Rules of Professional Conduct" from which the rules for individual states are derived.[4]

Like doctors and lawyers, faculty have a special relationship with their clients—their students. And while professors lack a similarly standardized code, the National Education Association's "Code of Ethics for Educators" is likely not too far off from the professional ethical obligations of faculty.[5] (Here I use "faculty" to refer broadly to educators within the university.) Professional ethics for faculty focuses on the fiduciary-like responsibilities we have toward our students—responsibilities above and beyond those we have to others.

I don't mean to assert that faculty are the *legal* fiduciaries of students in the United States. Though this has sometimes been held to be the case, in general faculty are not legal fiduciaries in the same way that you think of a financial adviser as *legally* being a fiduciary of a client.[6] But there's a sound argument that faculty are *ethical* fiduciaries of their students.[7] (For an extended discussion of the distinction between our ethical and legal obligations, see chapter 5.) We ought to make decisions that are in the best interest of our students, even if that is not always what the law requires of us. That means we are obligated to put the best interests of our students first and avoid conflicts of interest. Creating a conflict of interest is a violation of our professional duties to our students and the trust they place in us.

Investment in a student's start-up creates precisely such a conflict. It drives a wedge between student and educator, polluting the educator's pedagogical relationship with the potential for profit and in turn exploitation—even if the latter is not even remotely the intent.

One might argue that the university is *more* aligned with its students' interests when it invests in their start-ups. But while that may be true in a strictly financial sense, it is little different than when doctors use their own patients in clinical trials in which the physicians (or their hospitals) have a financial interest. Because the doctors have something to gain from the clinical trials, their care for the patients is drawn into question. Like those doctors, universities that act as investors introduce a conflict of interest into their relationship with their students.

These conflicts are apparent in the many questions a reasonable student might ask. (Asking what a *reasonable* student may think is perhaps too lax a criterion; in my administrative experience at Yale, I find it more useful to consider what an *unreasonable* observer may think.) Will student start-ups in which the university has a stake receive preferential treatment on campus? Will those start-ups be introduced more often to wealthy alumni or featured in school-sponsored social media? Will the students with those start-ups be more competitive for fellowships, mentorship programs, and other scarce resources at the university? If the university is an investor in a student start-up, to whose interests—students, founders, shareholders, or the company—will the university's educators tend to orient?

When universities invest in student start-ups—even if we're giving the students good terms—we are *using* those students—using them for *profit*. Indeed, profit is the whole point of investing. If universities didn't want a profit, we'd just *give* student entrepreneurs money and resources without strings attached.

If using students for profit sounds wrong to you, you're in good company. German philosopher Immanuel Kant (1724–1804) wrote, "Act so that you treat humanity, whether in your own person or in that of another, always as an end, and never as a mere means."[8] Kant comes up many times in this book, so a more formal introduction is warranted. He is a colossus of ethics. Kant considered morality not to be a set of rules handed down from on high by a deity or rules proscribed by the norms of our human society but rather that humanity's capacity for *reason*—our rationality—was the basis for morality.

In his *Groundwork of the Metaphysics of Morals*, Kant aimed to "seek out and establish the supreme principle of morality," which he called the *Kategorischer Imperativ* or "categorical imperative"—a single, overarching ethical principle from which all other ethical principles are derived: *one rule to rule them all*.[9]

Kant's categorical imperative is to "act only according to that maxim, through which you at the same time can will that it becomes a universal law."[10] Here a "maxim" is a rule for behaving, such as "I will steal to increase my wealth whenever I feel I cannot be caught." Kant believed that only those maxims that could be applied to all humanity—that is, *universalized*—form the basis for ethical action.

In *Groundwork*, Kant showed how prohibitions against stealing, lying, and other well-known transgressions can be derived from the categorical imperative. He also translated his categorical imperative into the roughly equivalent but more intuitive version that I mentioned previously: that we should treat people "always as an end, and never as a mere means."[11] Here Kant is saying that it is unethical to *use* other people merely to satisfy our own desires; it is our duty to treat others with respect and work for their happiness as well as our own.

The categorical imperative and its duties, for Kant, are unavoidable. All rational beings have an *imperative* to abide by it *categorically*, without exception or excuse. When the university invests in student start-ups, it risks running roughshod over Kant's categorical imperative by using students as a means—a means to profit—rather than doing what it ought to do, which is seeing to those students' education. (Kant exhorts us not to use others as a *mere* means—and here the word "mere" can necessitate a great deal of analysis.[12] Suffice it to say that the more we use people as a means without regard to what those people want, the more we find ourselves in ethical peril, from Kant's perspective.)

This risk of running roughshod over Kant's categorial imperative is not restricted to investing in student entrepreneurs. Universities can use or exploit their students in all sorts of ways. Think of the student athletes who rake in millions of dollars for universities without compensation, the students completing unpaid internships for school credit, and the students lured into PhD programs in English without any hope of finding an academic position after graduation.

Even if a university doesn't take equity in its start-ups, it still risks exploiting student entrepreneurs. This is because universities have indirect profits—the "externalities" of entrepreneurship activity on campus such as reputation gains, alumni engagement, improved faculty recruiting and retainment, increased employment opportunities for trailing faculty partners, IP licensing, sponsored research, and local economic development. As Mauri Laukkanen observed, universities are always at risk of making students "unwitting tools" in their pursuit of these ends.[13]

I am not arguing that universities should *not* support entrepreneurs. Indeed, I am paid to support entrepreneurs, and I spend a great deal of time convincing my colleagues in the Yale administration to devote *more* resources to entrepreneurship. What I am maintaining is that when we support entrepreneurs with *anything but their education* in mind, we face ethical peril, and so our best approach is simply to focus on our primary duty to students—education—and avoid the sorts of investments I've been discussing. We should *not* take equity in our students' ventures except—and even this should be prefaced with *perhaps*—in cases such as when a student venture receives something *extraordinary* like a patent license from the university and equity is received in lieu of other payment (discussed below).

My colleagues who demanded participation rights and other privileges from Emma and her fellow students in Yale's summer accelerator put themselves in the impossible position of being both investors and unconflicted educators. They created a textbook conflict of interest.

Inadequate Consent

When Emma came to see me about the Yale accelerator contract, her first question was, "What are these participation rights they want?"

She had no clue—and why would she? She had never founded a start-up or worked with investors. In contrast, my colleagues at the accelerator were trained, paid professionals twice her age. They *drafted* the contract she was asked to sign and knew the terms in and out. As I considered her question, it dawned on me that students are hopelessly outmatched in their dealings with the university.

Hard-nosed readers may object to that characterization. After all, university students are usually consenting adults in the legal sense. They are free *not* to take university investments. But that logic ignores the substantial power imbalance between students and the university, and the fiduciary-like obligations of educators to their students. Universities don't typically permit faculty to be romantically involved with students or have students pick up a professor's dry cleaning, even though a student might consent to such relationships. Furthermore, though student entrepreneurs are old enough to sign a contract we put in front of them, they don't always understand what they're signing. Indeed, we have *clear* evidence that student entrepreneurs are not competent counterparties in their entrepreneurship-related negotiations with the university—proof in the form of their choice to receive an education in entrepreneurship *from us.*

It's easy for a student founder with big dreams and dollar signs in their eyes to give away the store. In Emma's case, she didn't even know what *participation rights* were, much less how those rights would influence future rounds of financing. From what I gathered, most of her student colleagues invited to the summer accelerator were in the same boat.

Does that mean that the university should *never* enter into an agreement with a student or a student's start-up? No. But the university should be careful in doing so, in the same way a doctor would be careful obtaining the consent of a patient before using an experimental medical device. A student's signature is insufficient proof of consent. Instead, universities should seek a higher standard known as "full and free," "valid," or "informed" consent.[14] These terms describe a consent that is voluntary, informed, made competently, and sometimes made currently.[15] A student who gives that level of consent to a contract must understand the contract's "material circumstances, alternatives, and consequences," have reasonable alternatives, and enter into the contract without coercion.[16] This stringent standard of consent protects the well-being and autonomy of the consent giver, and makes ethical something that otherwise may not be, namely a dangerous medical procedure in the case of patients or introduction of a conflict of interest in the case of students.

It should be easy for educators to determine whether students are able to give their full and free consent. Just ask whether those students would receive an A grade were they to take an examination that probes their understanding of the "material circumstances, alternatives, and consequences" of the contract into which they are entering. For example, does the student understand the consequences of accepting $25,000 in convertible debt with a 35 percent discount, 5 percent interest, $3 million cap, and eighteen-month maturity?[17] How Kafkaesque it would be for a student to enter into a deal with the university as a condition of their participation in a summer accelerator, only to learn through the accelerator's instruction that the deal they signed was bad.

This higher level of consent precludes "browserwrap" agreements whereby a student's mere participation in an activity or use of a resource is interpreted as consenting to the terms.[18] That's the sort of "agreement" that says something like, "By participating in this program, you agree to the following terms." Further, full and free consent precludes contracts that border on "illusory promising" whereby the terms can be changed unilaterally by the university.[19] For instance, if the university's contract with a student entrepreneur claims that "the participating student agrees to abide by university policies" and the university is free to update those policies, then the student cannot know the consequences prior to commitment. There is nothing to prevent the university from changing its policies to state, say, that IP developed while student founders are on campus will be the property of the university.

Just to be clear, I am not arguing that such contracts will be unenforceable. Instead, I am contending that these kinds of contracts fall short of the free and full standard of consent that the university should seek when contracting with students, particularly when those contracts involve the transfer of securities.

In practice, the higher standard of consent is aided by ensuring that students entering contractual agreements with the university have legal counsel. Even that, though, it is not sufficient to achieve full and free consent; it is possible to have an attorney and still not understand the agreement to which you are bound. The university should want the student to have legal counsel and could even help defray the cost, but doing so can be problematic. For example, imagine that the university recommends local legal counsel for students who are signing up for an accelerator program administered by the university, and also that the university pays for those legal services. The lawyers' clients are the students, and yet the funds to pay the lawyers' fees will be coming from the university. How long will the university continue to recommend a firm that vigorously pursues the students' interests or is otherwise a pain? Who is the *true* client? (For a discussion of educators as intermediaries between student founders and service providers such as attorneys, see chapter 4.)

This discussion of consent is worth capping off by addressing just *how much* legal knowledge student entrepreneurs ought to possess before we give them the entrepreneurship education they desire. To be sure, students don't need to have a law degree before prototyping their first widget, but neither should they be complete rubes. Between these two boundary conditions is a spectrum of options that are, in various institutions and situations, appropriate. For example, you can imagine that students working on technology start-ups involving formal IP in a practice-oriented class have more need of legal education than students in theory-oriented classes.

The practice-oriented students are more likely to encounter legal questions imminently, and their welfare depends greatly on how those questions are answered; one cannot go back in time to file a patent or Section 83(b) tax election for their equity. Similarly, students in start-up hotbeds such as Silicon Valley are more likely to need legal education and suffer from its absence.

As educators, we should be using our expertise to intuit the likelihood of students' legal risk and prepare students appropriately. For me, in my beloved backwater of New Haven, an hour of boring legal lecture is fine for the average student. For my "advanced" students, more is warranted, as it would be if my students regularly bumped into venture capitalists like Stanford students do. (Would that it was so!)

Adverse Selection and Moral Hazard

While Emma had come to me with her questions about the university's demand for participation rights for her admission to a summer accelerator, some in her cohort (most not as talented as she) were similarly surprised and went directly to my colleagues. They wanted to know whether participation rights were negotiable or they could do the accelerator without giving up participation rights. They were told *no*, unequivocally.

Unbeknownst to Emma, I was speaking with another student who had been accepted into the accelerator, Wu Chang, the founder of a start-up that was doing *amazingly* well. Wu hardly needed Yale's help at all. She had raised a bunch of money for her hardware start-up already. I often felt like Wu met with me more out of courtesy than need. Whereas Emma was a good entrepreneur, Wu was *great*.

Wu had also asked my colleagues whether she could she participate in the Yale accelerator without giving the university fungible participation rights. Her existing investors were not keen to give away future investment rights, and so she was disinclined to join the accelerator if Yale insisted on participation rights. Emma had been told no, but Wu was told "sure": the participation rights were negotiable; the liquidity payment was negotiable; all of it was negotiable.

This double standard illustrated clearly what I long knew: the *best* entrepreneurs don't need the university's assistance. Frequently, they don't want the university's assistance (though they're always pleased to appear to receive the university's endorsement). I understood the double standard as promoting what economists call *adverse selection.*

University investment funds typically have less prestige and less to offer than private market alternatives. For example, full-service venture capital firms and top-tier accelerators will often have dramatically more experience than university funds; offer guidance from active board members and surround entrepreneurs with mentors; actively court other investors with whom they frequently coinvest; and reserve substantial follow-on funding.

Can a university fund or accelerator be as good as the best private market options? Mostly no. Instead, university funds are closer to the pejorative "dumb money." The student entrepreneurs most likely to produce financial returns—the "best" entrepreneurs—will have access to outside options: the best venture capital funds, accelerators, and other resources. University accelerators and investment funds are not getting the very best start-ups, the absolute cream of the crop; those already left school and are off into the real world, working with the pros. Why would they stick around to slum it with the junior varsity team?

With the "best" gone, the "rest" are then marginally more likely to avail themselves of the university's investment offerings. That's adverse selection.

I could see adverse selection in action with Wu's start-up. Wu was amazing; she was clearly off to the major leagues and therefore not super jazzed to stick around with student founders not nearly as successful as she. I see the same thing every semester: the private markets find our best founders and "poof," they're gone. Who's left? Regular founders—great people, but not necessarily with great ventures. Sure, there are a few who are great. But there's also a bunch working on ventures that are just so-so, and even a few that are clearly dead-ends. Why? Well, like most universities, most of our entrepreneurship support has a fixed number of slots; we give out six fellowships, have fifteen accelerator slots, and so on. Those slots must be filled.

The flaw with that system is that universities pretty frequently keep ventures alive that would wither and die in the private market. They're zombie companies—already dead, and they don't even know it.

Why is this a problem? It's a problem because the founders of those companies really should do something different. They could take a salaried job. They could work for another start-up. They could avail themselves of the substantial resources that exist at most universities for job placement. After all, once students graduate, for the most part, those resources are no longer available. Students certainly shouldn't be working on Dead-End-on-Demand-Sandwich-Delivery Inc. As professional educators, we have an ethical obligation to do what is in the students' best interest, and often what's in their best interest is *not* supporting their start-ups outside the classroom. It's a problem when we encourage students to do something that is detrimental to their well-being.

Economists have a term for that as well: "moral hazard," which occurs when a hazardous behavior is subsidized and therefore encouraged. Insurance is the classic example. An "invincible" youth might think, "I have good health insurance. Sure, I'll jump into that rock quarry for a swim." Insurance markets are filled with adverse selection and moral hazard.

The risk for universities is that by subsidizing student's pursuit of questionable ventures, we're encouraging them to forgo their many other, better opportunities. This is a disservice to our students and an ethical peril for the university that chooses to invest in student start-ups. Of course, universities aren't doing this out of malice but rather for good reasons: we care for our students; we recognize the pedagogical value of working on ventures, regardless of whether they fail; and we're generally enthusiastic about entrepreneurship. So we try to be supportive of student ventures. We give the students funds and other resources. We provide a safety net for students that does not exist in the real world. But by doing all of this, insulating student entrepreneurs from the "real world," we can unwittingly encourage them to pursue doomed ventures.

This happens a lot. A few years ago, I worked with a student team that was an obvious train wreck. It had too many founders, many internal disputes, and was outsourcing software development—and thus burning what little cash it had—before having done enough customer discovery. I knew this, and I was open with the students about my assessment of their start-up's fortunes.

The founders were graduating with top marks from their MBA programs. They could have won great-paying jobs in consulting, finance, midsize start-ups, or whatever. But because they won a post-graduate entrepreneurial fellowship, they decided to keep working on their venture after graduation. They skipped all the recruiting events at our school. While McKinsey, Goldman, and Google were visiting, they were elsewhere, laser focused on their venture.

That went OK for about three months, until all of a sudden they couldn't reach their next milestone and raise the money from investors. They persisted just long enough to miss out on recruiting at Yale. They were no longer students; they were unemployed.

You may read my tale about adverse selection and think, "OK, why not just invest in or support the *good* start-ups?" It's not that easy. Most start-ups fail.[20] The vast majority of venture capital firms can't beat the returns of the stock market on an absolute basis, much less a risk-adjusted one.[21] In other words, even paid professionals do not do a great job picking winners. A university that thinks it can do better than that is deluding itself.

There is something poetic and perverse in this moral hazard. We are condemned by our care for students and enthusiasm for entrepreneurship. The more we support them, the more we insulate them from the private market and greater number of zombie companies we end up keeping on life support. That's not good for the students. It's not good for the university. Indeed, it's not good for anyone.

Extraordinary Support

Before Emma applied to Yale's summer accelerator, she took several courses in entrepreneurship at Yale. We clearly didn't do as good a job in those courses as we should have because she should have emerged knowing about participation rights. In a few of the courses, Emma could work on her venture *in class*, such as by using problems her venture was facing as fodder for class projects. In one course, our Start-up Founder Practicum, Emma's coursework was *entirely* based on her venture. She also availed herself of many other resources at our university. She built prototypes in one of Yale's makerspaces. Emma used our library's database subscriptions for market research and to find investors. She met with her cofounders and investors in workspaces around campus.

My colleagues at Yale wanted a stake in Emma's venture in exchange for her entrance to a summer accelerator. But what about these other resources Emma used at Yale? What would they have said to a proposal that Emma and other student entrepreneurs give a stake in their ventures in exchange for their use of our libraries, databases, courses, makerspaces, and meeting rooms? These are expensive. Faculty salaries are expensive. Some databases are expensive. And our makerspaces are *really* expensive. Emma used all of those things to the benefit of her venture.

Of course, such a proposal is ridiculous. Emma *already paid for these resources.* Like every other student, Emma paid her tuition and hence could expect to avail herself of Yale's resources in the same way other students do. That she used these resources for her start-up is irrelevant. If a student conceives of a bestselling book in an English class, would we demand a fraction of that student's royalties? The university does not obligate its budding artists, athletes, thespians, and engineers to pay us a fraction of their future fortunes.

Yet I am occasionally confronted with colleagues who think student founders should pay up for *ordinary* resources at our university— resources that are part of what you pay for with tuition. I think they single out founders for two reasons. One is simply greed. There's a sense that student entrepreneurs could make a ton of money. Shouldn't the university get a bit? The other is that most founders have a rather simple mechanism for sharing their wealth: *equity*. No other students have anything even remotely similar. The university's artists and athletes don't have stock we can take. For student entrepreneurs, however, it's *easy* to get a piece of their future wealth.

Easy, yes—but usually it's the wrong thing to do.

The university does not deserve, nor should it demand, equity from students who use university resources to which they are entitled by virtue of their tuition. Nor should we demand equity in cases where an entrepreneur receives the university's support, and that support is on par with that given to other constituencies on campus. For example, many universities spend substantial sums on student athletes, some of whom go on to be multimillionaires playing for professional sports teams.[22] We don't get a stake in their future fortunes. Universities have many fellowships and scholarships for students who excel, and we don't get a stake of *those* students' future fortunes. The summer accelerator to which Emma was admitted falls into this category. It was a program not so different from others on campus, such as in-residence summer fellowships for talented student musicians, thespians, or artists.

You might argue that entrepreneurs are different because they are involved in *for-profit* enterprises and therefore ought not be treated like the musicians on campus. First of all, musicians absolutely want to make money. Second, many student founders work on nonprofits or even for-benefit corporations. Within these categories, student founders are divided still. Some are working on scalable, venture-backable companies. Others are working on lifestyle companies. Some are organized as corporations; others are partnerships, sole proprietorships, organized abroad, or not organized at all. Some are working with cofounders at the same university, while others are working with far-flung cofounders. Some founded their companies in school, and some before. Some have traction; some do not.

This diversity makes charging for the ordinary resources of the university untenable—even if such a thing was ethically defensible. Imagine the problems my colleagues faced when they asked student entrepreneurs for a stake in their ventures. How would they treat cofounders who enroll in the program together? Do they owe twice as much equity? What if a student switches ideas, giving up the venture in which the university owns a stake. Ought the university own part of the *new* venture? How similar must it be? Another issue could arise if the founder who participates already has millions in funding, paying customers, or other substantial progress. Will this student receive a discount because the program will be less valuable to them? And what if the program's pedagogy is particularly poor due to new instruction; will students owe the university less?

You can see that even if it was "right" to charge students for ordinary resources at the university, which it is not, doing so is untenable. All students should be permitted equal access to the ordinary resources of the university. We ought not single out entrepreneurs. Instead, we ought to be happy when they use the resources of the university *to which they are entitled* and go on to be successful.

Shrewd readers will notice that there are, of course, ordinary things for which universities *do* charge students on the margin, like lunch plans, a locker in the gym, and so on. The charges for these things, however, are almost always roughly equal to the *marginal costs* of those things. A student doesn't risk accidentally paying a million dollars for a gym locker. But when a university takes equity, that is precisely what students risk.

Imagine ten student founders receive some ordinary resource from the university for which, in exchange, the university demands equity. Most of those founders will end up paying roughly zero for that resource because their start-up's equity will be worthless (most start-ups fail). Yet one or two students will end up paying *enormous* sums. There is simply no other context on campus in which such an exchange is acceptable, and it ought not be in the case for our student founders.

Certainly, it is possible for the university, if it so wished, to give extraordinary support to a student entrepreneur. Consider this hypothetical: a university invests a million dollars into a student start-up to fund business activities such as sales, clinical trials, software development, and so on. It's difficult to spot a pedagogical benefit to the student. No other students on campus receive comparable sums. The scale of the investment is large, and no student could reasonably expect to be the beneficiary of such largess merely through matriculation, timely payment of tuition, or excellence in their studies. Moreover, such an investment does little to further the teaching and research missions shared by most universities. I believe most readers would agree that a million-dollar injection of capital is *extraordinary* and the university making such an investment may reasonably expect recompense. (Though, again, I don't think such an investment is a good idea.)

While a million-dollar investment is rare, other forms of extraordinary support for student start-ups are more common, particularly patent licenses, research on a start-up's behalf, and use of specialized scientific equipment. No student could rationally expect to use a multimillion-dollar telescope or nuclear magnetic resonance spectrometer simply as an automatic by-product of having paid their tuition. To be granted a patent license or use of specialized research equipment is truly extraordinary.

I'm not certain where the line between ordinary and extraordinary is, but we can estimate it. Following a path from a million-dollar investment (or similarly valuable extraordinary resource) to a *zero-dollar* one, we would pass the median size of preseed investments by professional venture capitalists and the median size of grants in private start-up accelerators, arriving at sums so small that they would do little in furtherance of a student's start-up. The median investment sizes of accelerators and seed investors are clearly thought to be useful; the furtherance of a start-up is the *purpose* of these programs. A recent study shows that the mean minimum investment made by start-up accelerators is roughly $25,000.[23] (Many accelerators choose to invest further in "winners," so the mean total investment is somewhat higher.) This seems to me a reasonable threshold for an extraordinary amount in the sense that this amount is provided by private investors having profit rather than pedagogical priorities. In the absence of promises to the contrary, it is not reasonable for a student at most universities to expect receipt of such sums—*in cash* rather than *in-kind*—merely because that student paid tuition or excelled in their studies. A university providing such sums to a student entrepreneur would create the sort of conflict of interest I described earlier. Still, if the university asked the student founder for equity, the university would *not* be at risk of charging the student for that which the student already paid.

Even Ethics Aside, Investing Doesn't Make Sense

Imagine that you don't accept any of the foregoing ethical arguments I made. It still doesn't make much sense for a university to be investing in its student start-ups. As research shows, "there is an emerging consensus that average returns of VC [venture capital] funds do not exceed market returns."[24] The average venture fund achieves just 103 to 120 percent of the return provided by a broad basket of US public equities, net of venture fund fees and carried interest.[25] And the *real, risk-adjusted* return is even less because start-ups are riskier than public companies.

It gets worse. Most of the industry's returns are captured by just a handful of firms. These elite firms—Sequoia Capital, Andreessen Horowitz, Kleiner Perkins, and a few others—benefit from a powerful positive feedback loop: early success attracts the best partners, limited partners, and founders, who predispose the firm to success in future years.[26] What an advantage! Even without the potential ethical considerations, a fund run by modestly compensated university staff investing in a small pool of student start-ups is not so lucky.

While it's difficult for a university to make money investing in its students' start-ups, it is easy to ruin opportunities for others to do so. It's a perversion economists call "crowding out," which happens when public or university support for entrepreneurs *replaces* private market support rather than enhancing it.[27] Why would an angel group spring up in your university town if the university is already funding student start-ups?

Those who are tempted to pursue profit by investing in student ventures should remember that most of the returns in venture capital are captured by only small number of "winning" firms. Among the "losers" are vast numbers of reputable firms, staffed by experienced investment professionals, who ardently pursue and ultimately fail to find the almighty dollar in their start-up investments. Can a university do better than those so-called losers by investing in its students' start-ups? *Perhaps* a few dozen universities could. But for the median university, it seems doubtful and unwise, even putting the ethical considerations aside.

*   *   *

Investing in our students' start-ups is a moral minefield that is best avoided. When we choose profit over pedagogy, we fail in our professional duties to students and risk making them our unwitting tools.

The good news is that avoiding this minefield is easy. We would be wise to heed the words of Robert Maynard Hutchins (1899–1977), who was dean of Yale Law School before becoming president and chancellor of the University of Chicago. In his book *The Higher Learning in America* (1995), Hutchins wrote,

> It is a good principle of educational administration that a college or university should do nothing that another agency can do as well. This is a good principle because a college or university has a vast and complicated job if it does what only it can do.[28]

Universities should focus on teaching and research, and leave investing to the investors.

Recommendations:

- The university should ensure that its support of student entrepreneurs is modest, comparable to support offered to other students, and in furtherance of entrepreneurs' *education* rather than their ventures.

- The university should avoid financial interests in student start-ups except in the cases wherein a student start-up receives extraordinary resources, such as a patent license, and the university receives securities in lieu of cash payment.

- To encourage the founding of student start-ups—and rather than directly investing—the university should create an environment in which private investors and students can easily find each other, with numerous opportunities for small, positive interactions. We should have venture capitalists roaming the hallways; we should not be competing with venture capitalists or acting as their gatekeepers on campus. If the university feels that not enough capital is available, it should invest in local venture capitalists rather than investing in start-ups directly.

3
Faculty Investment and Involvement in Student Start-ups

I teach a class at Yale called Start-up Founder Studies. It's a delightful class in which we discuss "advanced" aspects of the start-up founding experience and read a modicum of entrepreneurship research literature, and I invite guests to class—typically experienced founders or investors—to help us understand how what we're learning in *theory* is manifest in *practice*. Though the class is mostly for graduate students and exclusively for students who are experienced founders, I make a habit of admitting precocious undergraduates—like a junior named Lisa, who was in the course a few years ago.

Lisa was a joy to have in class. She asked perceptive questions and was quick with (generally correct) answers. She also sought my advice outside class. Like most faculty, I am not obliged to give students my time outside the classroom, but I try to do so. In particular, I love to help founders of technology ventures because even more than entrepreneurship, I like coding and talking to people about code. Lisa was a tech founder, so she and I had a lot to talk about. I felt I helped her a great deal, and she felt so too.

Toward the end of our semester, Lisa told me she earned a spot in a prestigious Silicon Valley accelerator where she would spend her summer with her cofounder, who was a graduating senior. Lisa expressed her gratitude for all of my help and asked whether I would accept a small bit of equity as an expression of that gratitude.

She also told me that she would soon raise an angel round, and be even more grateful if I'd consider investing in and remaining an adviser to her company.

I suspect my experience with Lisa will sound familiar to many entrepreneurship educators who, like me, are in the enviable positions of being surrounded by bright young student founders. These founders often ask us to become board members or consultants. They offer gifts, such as the gift of equity Lisa offered me, or compensation for our service. And they frequently ask us to invest in their companies. Should we avail ourselves of these opportunities? That is the $10,000 question—or maybe even the $1 million question.[1]

The Appeal

Let me tell you as an entrepreneurship educator, what I find appealing about investing in or getting involved with student ventures outside the classroom—for example, as a board member, adviser, or consultant. It begins with a simple fact: student founders are often long on enthusiasm but short on cash. We know that access to capital increases with age, but most student founders are young, and I might be one of the few accredited investors they know and trust.[2] I would feel good being the "first dollar in," to have helped the cash-strapped student when they needed it most.

I believe it is fair to say that I also have some usefulness beyond my ability to write a check. Like most entrepreneurship educators, I am well-connected. My job makes me a nexus through which people with an interest in entrepreneurship meet. I know tons of recently graduated students who might work for a start-up. I know hundreds of wealthy alumni. I know loads of angel investors and venture capitalists. Someday, my students will have extensive professional networks and ready access to capital, but that's not the case for most of them today. So I'm a handy person to have on board.

And it's not just that I know helpful people; I think I am helpful in my own right. I've sold a few ventures, I know a lot about building software, and my advice is decent. For those reasons and more, I think I make a desirable adviser, investor, or board member for a student entrepreneur just starting out.

Of course, some students don't give a hoot about my cash or other utility; they just want to be able to say, "My professor invested." It's social proof or "signaling." Faculty investment and involvement in a student venture is a positive signal for investors because "highly regarded scholars would not commit their wealth and reputation to ventures with low expectations for success."[3]

That's spot-on. I have privileged information about the student ventures in my classes and therefore a good sense of who is apt to excel—on top of which, I'm not keen to stake my "wealth and reputation," such as it is, on the others. So if a student says truthfully that I invested, I'm on the start-up's board, I'm working with the development team, or I otherwise have "skin in the game," investors should take it as a positive signal. In fact, it's a *ringing endorsement.*

This endorsement, or signal, that I can send through my investment and involvement with student ventures is potentially appreciated not only by students but also by professional investors. By watching which students I invest in, professional investors could better discern which of my university's start-ups are worthy. So you can imagine that by investing in my students, I am cultivating a thriving, meritocratic local investment market—something I very much wish to see.

Well-functioning markets do a reasonably good job of allocating resources. They're not perfect, but we don't know of a better way to allocate capital than allowing unfettered market participants to pick and choose how to do so themselves.[4] Key to that is information, and entrepreneurship educators are well-informed market participants. To the extent that they may refrain from investing in student ventures, they are depriving other market participants of the wisdom of their judgments.

Investing in student start-ups is a potentially lucrative activity too. Some of my students' ventures, for instance, become worth hundreds of millions of dollars. Some become unicorns. Some go public. Some get acquired. Often, an equity stake wouldn't set me back much; Lisa isn't the only one of my students who wanted just to *give* me equity. Some founders might require my time and effort, but usually not much. A good fraction of students most desire the aforementioned *signal* my involvement provides—they just want my smiling face on their website or in their pitch deck. So with little work, my inside edge thanks to privileged information, and relatively generous terms from grateful graduates, I feel as if I could do pretty well financially—and like most people, I'd enjoy being wealthier.

The final reason I want to invest in or otherwise involve myself with my students' start-ups is that *it just seems fun*. I love teaching entrepreneurship, but I miss being a founder. Watching my students run their start-ups feels, in some ways, like watching my kids play soccer and other sports. I think, "Hey, let me try. Watch how it's done." I'm pretty sure I could run my students' start-ups better than they can. (And I would certainly excel on a soccer field filled with ten-year-old kids.) My rational side knows I would never have time to get deeply involved in the day-to-day operations of a bunch of student start-ups. But still, sitting on the sideline stinks. I want to get back into the game.

My Role and Its Duties

So should I become involved with my students' start-ups as an investor, board member, or consultant? Despite my foregoing arguments, which I find compelling, the answer for me is *no*. Many educators reach the opposite conclusion.[5]

My decision not to invest or become involved with my students' start-ups is not for lack of interest, financial capacity, or opportunity to do so—as I've already made clear. It is instead because I believe such involvement is incompatible with my role as an educator.

I remember my early entrepreneurial life as a graduate student and founder at MIT, when I felt a nebular unease around the faculty and staff who made a habit of investing in or involving themselves with student ventures. Those educators, I felt, had favorites, and those start-up teams—even if they weren't in my market—competed with me for prizes and other scarce resources that the educators dispensed. I recall feeling that some educators expected their rings to be kissed in exchange for introductions to investors or access to university resources they controlled. (For a discussion of faculty as intermediaries between students and service providers such as investors and attorneys, see chapter 4.) In short, when I was a student founder, I did not trust educators who became overly involved with student ventures.

Only now, sitting on the other side of the table as an entrepreneurship educator, do I understand what triggered that lack of trust. The student Kyle of yesteryear did not know, when he met with a given professor, whether he was meeting with Professor Smith the educator or Professor Smith the potential angel investor. Professor Smith had blurred the lines between those roles, and in so doing, lost my trust.

The roles of educator and investor are in conflict, as Bill Aulet—well-known as the managing director of the Martin Trust Center for MIT Entrepreneurship (at this writing) and his book *Disciplined Entrepreneurship*—has observed. He asks,

> Do the students look at us as educators who are there for their
> personal development or are we investors . . . ? Should they be open
> and honest with us or should they try to impress us so they get us as

investors? What happens to those we do not invest in, what signal does that send to the broader market? The moment we are something other than 100 percent educators is the day we lose our "honest broker" uniqueness. . . . Being an honest broker educator to me means that we are always completely looking out for our students' best interests.[6]

As Aulet observed, I cannot invest in my student's ventures while upholding my fiduciary-like duties to my students, or in his words, being an "honest broker." Kyle the educator and Kyle the investor are different people with different, incompatible roles.

A "role," in the sociological sense, is a constellation of virtues exhibited by, rights bestowed to, and duties incumbent on an individual in light of their position in a social network.[7] Though there are similarities, it is one thing to be a virtuous or excellent faculty member—to teach well and command the research literature—and another thing to be a virtuous or excellent investor.[8] And just as the virtues of educators and investors are different, so are the rights and duties of people in these roles. For example, an educator may have access to the faculty lounge and the protection of tenure. An investor may have rights to information or voting in the affairs of a start-up. Most important is that the duties of these roles differ. As faculty, I have the duty to educate students and look after their best interests. As investor, I have a duty to provide returns to my general partners or myself.

The heterogeneous duties of roles form the basis of "role ethics," which has been a significant genre of ethics since the times of Confucius and Epictetus.[9] Should you break down a person's door? Generally, no—but if you're a firefighter, you might have a duty to do so. Is it OK to keep your silence in order to spare someone's feelings? Sure, unless you're a physician withholding a diagnosis. Through our roles, we acquire duties we otherwise lack. Role ethics is the study of those duties. It helps us know right from wrong, not replacing our ordinary morality, but building on it through consideration of our social roles, which are "central to determining what we ought to do."[10]

Of course, all of us occupy multiple roles. I am faculty, a parent, and have at times been a board member of companies and nonprofits. Some roles come to us naturally, such as "daughter" or "citizen"; some, like "attorney," are acquired through explicit agreements; and still others we acquire through tacit agreements.[11] The *professions* are a special type of role (introduced in chapter 2); not all roles are professions, but all professions are, in the parlance of role ethics and sociology, roles. Persons in professional roles are generally held to a high ethical standard, particularly vis-à-vis those they serve in their professional capacities—their clients. For instance, professionals like doctors, therapists, and professors are *fiduciaries* of their clients, as discussed in chapter 2, and have a duty not to introduce conflicts of interest into their relationships with those clients.

"Faculty member" is a good example of what Robert Merton, one of the founders of modern sociology, called a "role set"; it is a complicated set of roles that we bundle under one heading.[12] Think of all the aspects of being faculty: faculty qua educator, faculty qua scholar, faculty qua career adviser. Most of these aspects of our jobs exist harmoniously; when they conflict—such as when we want to run an experiment on students in our classes—universities have mechanisms for managing potential issues. Sometimes, however, a person in multiple roles creates a "role conflict" due to the *"relative incompatibility* of expectations between roles."[13] In a role conflict, one brings the virtues, rights, and duties from one domain into another—an act that "generates surprise, uneasiness, disappointment, or disapproval."[14]

Surprise, uneasiness, and disappointment—and ultimately disapproval—are all apt descriptions of how I felt as a student about the Janus-faced faculty with personal interests in student start-ups. Those educators developed role conflicts; they had "dual roles" or "dual relationships" with their students, thus "simultaneously or sequentially participating in two role categories that conflict or compete."[15]

The roles of entrepreneurship educator and investor are, for me, in an irreconcilable conflict when it comes to student start-ups. I don't feel I can, at once, be both educator and investor in the start-up of my own student and fulfill my professional obligations—my duties—to my students, or to a lesser extent, my employer, the university. (Of course, it's totally fine and even good for me to be investing in start-ups away from campus. My focus here is on entrepreneurship educators investing in student start-ups.) In chapter 2, I contend that universities generally ought not invest in student ventures. Many of the arguments from that chapter apply *mutatis mutandis* to the case of individual entrepreneurship educators investing in their personal capacities—although I believe the educator-student case is most intuitively understood in terms of role ethics and role conflicts, as I described above. Let's look more closely at the nuances of these conflicts.

Power Asymmetries

Most faculty intuitively know that they should not develop business relationships with their *current students* primarily because of the immense power faculty have over students.[16]

The power over grading is most glaring, as some of the questions it poses illustrate. If I was an equity investor in one of my student's ventures, would I lose my objectivity? Would I grade them leniently—consciously or not—or give them more attention than other students? Would I allow the student to work on a project that was not scholarly but instead furthered my financial interests? Would I use my classroom power over the student to gain some advantage in our business affairs? Would I encourage a student to drop out of school so that they could work full time on the venture in which I've

invested? Such conflicts of interest are clear violations of the professional duties faculty have to students. So for most faculty, it is self-
evident—and axiomatic even—that investing in current students is
best avoided.[17]

What I think is less obvious is that even assiduous professors investing only in, say, *recent graduates* are also at risk of abusing their power.
Imagine that I have a policy of not investing in current students, but
allow myself to do so right after students graduate. What is to prevent me from "grooming" my students for investment while they
are in class with me or otherwise under my sway? Would students
perceive me as objective? Likely not; they would rightly perceive me
as both faculty and potential investor. In such a case, would my students disclose to me their setbacks and failures freely, as would most
benefit their education? Some student founders might opt instead to
withhold unflattering data, knowing I am a potential investor.

Further, if I am an investor—potential or actual—how are students to know that my advice is in *their* best interest and not in
the service of *my* interests? As one scholar wrote, "Because of the
asymmetry in the relationship, we cannot assume that persons
interacting with the professional are able to objectively evaluate the
advice of the professional and reject it when it is not in their best
interests."[18]

Dual relationships—role conflicts—also have *negative externalities* that affect students and educators alike. Professor Smith making
a habit of investing in students raises questions about their own
objectivity *and* that of other faculty. It's a risk that exists even if Professor Smith is *in fact* totally objective; the "perceived loss of objectivity may be just as damaging as the actual loss of objectivity."[19]

Consider the case of the Stanford mobile payment start-up Clinkle, which was "funded in part by professors, and the university's
president" immediately following the three founders' graduation
from the university. The start-up had close ties to the university,
including employing numerous students.

Clinkle raised complicated questions about values and conflicts: Do students get good grades if they start a company that their professors invest in? What happens to a student who wants to create a competitor to a company the chair of his department has already helped fund? Professors have coercive power, which isn't the best thing to pair with financial opportunity.[20]

Stanford University's president invested in that start-up. It is difficult to fathom a more auspicious social signal for the founders. But what of the next mobile payment start-up? Would the president fund it too?

The Clinkle story reminds me of when I was in third grade and brought candy to class. My teacher chastised me; bringing candy to school is fine, she told me, as long as I bring enough for *everyone*. I doubt Stanford's president was bringing enough proverbial candy for every student who might want or need some. If the president of a university makes a habit of investing in student ventures, even after graduation, what is the effect of that precedent on other students? I think it would lead investors to ask future entrepreneurs who graduated from that university whether the president invested in *their* start-ups.

Even if the objectivity of a university president and their faculty were *in truth* maintained in making such investments, the *perception* of that objectivity would be shattered. Student founders in that environment will rightly question whether educators have students' best interests at heart.

Another reason to avoid investing in recent graduates is that it likely inhibits their development. Students ought to be kicked out of the nest so they learn to fend for themselves. As one scholar noted, "The educational goal is for students to develop their own competence, not to develop a dependency on having a 'special' relationship with a faculty member."[21] To fund our students is to stunt their development and perpetuate dependency on the expertise, networks, and other resources of their educators.

Funding and support from faculty may also create a moral hazard if we support students or recent graduates more generously than the cold, calculating capitalists of the private market. I am sheepish to admit that this is a transgression of which I'm guilty—though I've since learned from my errors. My most egregious case was with the charming but hapless Elijah, a student committed to a hopeless construction start-up. I panicked when he told me he had turned down a well-paid consulting job to work on his venture, and I did something for him that I had never done before: I got involved with his venture and built his "minimum viable product" with my own hands. I spent dozens of hours writing software for him that he could deploy to the cloud provider of his choice and use for his customer discovery efforts—code I *gave* to Elijah without charge.

French fabulist Jean de La Fontaine wrote, "Our destiny is frequently met in the very paths we take to avoid it."[22] Such was my experience with Elijah. My fears for Elijah's welfare compelled me to "help" him. But I fear this help merely created a moral hazard, encouraged his folly, and prolonged the inevitable. For years he proceeded with difficulty, just as hapless and his venture just as hopeless as on the first day. I ought not to have intervened.

Duties to the University

I once knew a licensing officer at a prestigious university who negotiated the terms of a patent license with a university spin-off. Subsequently, as I understand it, this licensing officer joined the company's board to champion the university's continuing interests. Years passed, and having found a modicum of success, the company filed an S-1 with the Securities and Exchange Commission in preparation for a public offering. That S-1 revealed that the licensing officer—in consideration of their board service—was *personally* issued stock worth hundreds of thousands of dollars. Their university colleagues were understandably bewildered and curious, wondering whether this licensing officer had used the power of the university to obtain a personally lucrative board seat and how faithfully they had pursued the university's interests. Should each of the university's start-ups invite the university's licensing offers and other power brokers to their boards, hoping for favorable terms to their IP licenses?

I think about this story often. While it's not about an entrepreneurship educator per se, licensing officers and entrepreneurship educators are quite similar: each of us has wide exposure to many ventures on campus and latitude to deploy the university's resources in support of those ventures.

This licensing officer controlled access to the university's IP. In my role, I control classes, scholarships, fellowships, grants, and other resources. I could, rather easily, use these resources to my advantage, directing them to campus start-ups that have the potential to enrich me rather than using those resources for the fulfillment of the university's mission. I might even do that unconsciously.

As Greek statesman Demosthenes said, "Nothing is easier than to deceive oneself."[23] It would be easy for me, in many cases as an entrepreneurship educator, to deceive myself into thinking that the very thing that benefits me is the right thing to do. For example, I know entrepreneurship educators who tell me that they take seats on the boards of student companies to *protect* those naive student founders from professional investors to whom students might otherwise fall prey. Instead, the potential for my benefit—whether financial, reputational, or otherwise—should be an alarm, a prompt for caution. Where there is potential for my benefit, there is also the potential that I am being a poor steward of the resources entrusted to me by my university.

Information is a particularly precious resource to which educators are privy. "Students often reveal sensitive information to professors, as they might to a therapist or a medical doctor, and they trust professors not to use this information to exploit them," writes Belinda Blevins-Knabe.[24] That accurately describes *my* experience with student founders: they tell me all the "dirt." Indeed, I frequently *compel* student founders to do so in my classes; they could not get a good grade without intense open discussions about their ventures. If I use that information to make an investment decision, I have wronged the student—akin to my therapist using private information about me to recommend that I not be admitted to a local pool club.

Less obvious is that this is also a betrayal of our duties to our universities for two reasons. One, the university empowers us as educators to demand privileged information from student ventures. The university has a reasonable expectation that its educators use that information for the furtherance of the university's mission and not misappropriate the information for personal gain—just as corporations expect employees to use privileged corporate information for the furtherance of the corporation's goals and not insider trading.

The other is that to the extent that the misappropriation of private information about student ventures adversely affects students' education, I have done my job poorly and failed in my duties to my employer. As I wrote earlier, even the *perception* of misusing information is enough to erode students' trust in educators and thereby impair students' education.

Like private information about student ventures, there are other resources I accrue in my role as entrepreneurship educator, but that are not formally vested in me by the university. My *network* is the most notable. For instance, through my role, I have come to know scores of investors, including wealthy alumni and venture capitalists. I have a valuable social network, which is one reason student founders ask me to sit on their boards or otherwise be involved with their start-ups. Student founders are willing to *pay* for access to my network—and I know of some entrepreneurship faculty who *do* charge their students for access to *their* networks, such as by charging students for introductions to investors (see chapter 4).

That seems both acquisitive and perverse. The lion's share of my social network exists because of my role in the university. A replacement faculty member would sit in my same room in my same university building and acquire *roughly* my same social network. That is to say, even though my social network is not the property of the university, I acquired it due to my role—and it seems perverse to deny that asset to the students who ought to benefit from my role. I should instead, to a first approximation, think of my social network the same way I think of the scholarship funds in my control: I ought to use it for the furtherance of the university's mission rather than private gain, at least with regard to my students.

Faculty as Technical Cofounders

I now address a substantial elephant in the room: the common case of faculty—usually science, technology, engineering, and medicine (STEM) faculty, not entrepreneurship educators—who are technical cofounders with students they also supervise. (By "technical cofounders," I mean those founders of a venture focused on the technology that enables a product. They are distinct from, say, "business cofounders," who are focused more broadly on product design, customer discovery, sales, operations, financing, and the like.) I must do so in a way that is not completely satisfactory for the simple reason that this book is about entrepreneurship education and educators, not faculty in other quarters of the university, and so space does not allow for anything more than a brief overview of the conflicts presented by STEM faculty cofounding ventures with their students.

(Indeed, the roles of faculty adviser and cofounder are full of conflicts worthy of thoughtful exposition—which, alas, would easily fill an entire book. Another elephant in the room is the case of part-time, practitioner faculty and mentors involved with student ventures. You will find that discussion in chapter 4.)

Imagine a faculty-student pair that patents and commercializes something developed as part of the student's PhD thesis. Such ventures are the bread and butter of university entrepreneurship and contribute mightily to the many "secondary gains" of universities with respect to entrepreneurship, particularly faculty retention and local economic development. Universities *want* STEM faculty to start companies with students based on innovative research.

Of course, that dual relationship is dicey; a PhD student and faculty adviser starting a company together are in a serious role conflict—one in which the adviser has a lot of power. How voraciously will the student be able to argue with an adviser about IP or equity if the student requires the adviser's signature to graduate? I can answer from my personal experience as that student: *not voraciously at all.*

On most campuses, STEM faculty are among the most important and successful entrepreneurs. Having said that, I think many universities do a woeful job of managing the conflicts introduced by faculty-student ventures. I believe universities accept the role conflict produced by STEM faculty-student ventures for consequentialist reasons. In other words, universities believe there is more to be gained than lost. These ventures often bring lifesaving, world-changing technologies to the masses, and for that reason, universities tolerate and even encourage faculty to cofound ventures with students despite the fact that doing so creates a serious role conflict.

I should explain this *consequentialism* and its best-known form, utilitarianism, a bit more because it comes up many times in discussions of the ethics of entrepreneurship education. "Utilitarianism" is the normative ethical theory that says we ought to do whatever actions bring about the most utility in the world. In this specific context, the word "utility"—which economists love—basically means people's welfare, namely the degree to which they experience pleasure and avoid pain or suffering.

Sixteenth-century English philosopher Jeremy Bentham was one of the first to articulate this form of ethical thinking. He wrote,

> Nature has placed mankind under the governance of two sovereign masters, pain and pleasure. It is for them alone to point out what we ought to do. . . . On the one hand the standard of right and wrong, on the other the chain of causes and effects, are fastened to their throne. They govern us in all we do, in all we say, in all we think.[25]

Most famously, he said, "The greatest happiness of the greatest number is the foundation of morals and legislation."[26]

This genre of ethical theories is one in which what makes an action right or wrong is not an innate duty or mental state, as Kant would say, but rather the *consequences* of our actions. In the words of English philosopher John Stuart Mill, who (with small differences) expanded on Bentham's philosophy a generation later, "Actions are right in proportion as they tend to promote happiness, wrong as they tend to produce the reverse of happiness."[27]

Utilitarianism is appealing because it is so conceptually simple. It is, however, tricky too—in a few ways that are quite well-known. First, it's tough to know the full consequences of our actions on others and easy to justify that which may be in our own interests. For example, exaggerating the merits of a venture perhaps seems to bring about the best consequences, but *from my perspective.* Consequentialist thinking can also run roughshod over individual rights. A consequentialist might, say, justify giving an experimental drug to unwitting patients in order to advance science.

For all of my talk of role ethics, professional ethics, and Kant, I agree—on consequentialist grounds—that universities ought to permit STEM faculty to cofound ventures with their students. I cannot imagine a modern university in which such relationships are prohibited. But universities should manage the potential for conflicts. For instance, when a student cofounds a company with their adviser, the university could add an extra faculty member to the student's thesis committee to act as a "conflict manager." This committee member could ensure that a student's thesis is not perverted, and to some extent, that the adviser's power does not disadvantage the student, either in the context of the nascent company or the student's progress toward graduation.

Universities can also ensure that faculty-student teams are educated about potential conflicts, the basics of entrepreneurial law, and entrepreneurial finance. A student and adviser should know how best to reach an agreement over splitting equity. Do they know what fraction of equity a faculty person *typically* receives if they are not leaving their academic post to join the company? Basic education in these subjects can ameliorate the impact of the power imbalance between student and adviser.

Finally, universities should insist that faculty *and students* report commercial activity that might impinge on students' education. The university shouldn't preclude that activity—indeed, we want to stimulate it—but instead use reporting as the gateway to training and engagement.

None of these suggestions are a panacea, but each one is a step in the right direction. It's a shame that most universities do almost nothing to manage the conflicts of interest inherent in student-adviser start-ups. Surely *something* is possible—and advisable.

If, despite the clear role conflicts, I condone STEM faculty-student ventures on consequentialist grounds, you might rightly ask, by what logic do I disapprove of entrepreneurship educators investing in or becoming involved with student ventures? I think the involvement of STEM faculty with the companies founded by their students is almost *necessary*, whereas the same can only rarely be said of entrepreneurship faculty's involvement. My colleague, a professor in electrical engineering, recently started an LED company with one of his students based on their research. How many people in this world could replace the professor in this company? You can count them on your hands. He is basically irreplicable and nonsubstitutable. In contrast, the skills that I bring to a company as an entrepreneurship educator are more widely found. I am easily substituted and thus have less of an "excuse" to wade into a role conflict.

Beyond that, a single STEM faculty person is likely involved with one or perhaps two ventures on campus (although outliers exist) and hence the fallout from role conflicts is limited. In contrast, entrepreneurship educators have wide exposure to ventures on campus and therefore the potential fallout from their role conflicts is widespread.

Best Practices and Exceptions

The roles of entrepreneurship educator and investor are irredeemably in conflict. Educators who invest only in students after graduation do not escape this conflict. They are still at risk of abusing their power by grooming students for investment prior to graduation or being perceived as doing so. But this danger, and the power of faculty over students and recent alums, is not everlasting. As Arlene McCormack writes, "The degree of power that the teacher has over the student increases the more the student wants to attain a goal mediated by the teacher and decreases as the availability of reaching these goals outside the relationship increases."[28]

Entrepreneurship educators are, I believe, very much the mediators of goals for student entrepreneurs. I am a gatekeeper and steward of the university's immense capacity to support student ventures. I have great power over student founders. But what is my power—my leverage—over a student who graduated ten years ago? It is not zero, yet it is much diminished and close to zero. It is, I think, reasonable to assume that such an alumnus seeking my investment does not *need* it; they have alternatives. And if they offer me the chance to invest in their company, they do so without the risk that I've coerced them or abused the power vested in me by the university. As such, in most respects, it would be *fine* for me to invest in or involve myself with the venture of this alumnus.

If a ten-year absence from campus is enough for a student to gain their independence from my power, what about five years? One year? One day? *I don't know the answer*, but it may vary by student, educator, and school, and I suspect it is measured in years and not months.

For other citizens on campus, a shorter wait to invest is likely fine. For example, imagine if a member of our facilities staff wished to invest in a student start-up. This person is not an educator per se but absolutely supports the educational enterprise of our university. The staff member likely has little to no power over a student founder and therefore bears little risk of a role conflict; this person's role in the university and as an investor are compatible. Similarly, a professor of Modern Hebrew might invest in the venture of an MBA student with few risks because the professor would have little power over the MBA student who is not in the professor's department. I'm not saying these are *smart* decisions, just that they are less ethically delicate than the case of the entrepreneurship educator investing in student start-ups.

Entrepreneurship educators are different. We should not think of ourselves as players in "the game" of university entrepreneurship. Instead, we ought to think of ourselves as the coaches or referees. Maybe we're also the groundskeepers. We are the people in the university who help create an environment in which *others* thrive— particularly students, but other faculty as well. We are best served by staying out of the game. The same goes for licensing professionals and university administrators such as deans, presidents, and the staff of programs supporting campus entrepreneurship, all of whom possess sizable power over student start-ups.

That is not to say that educators and administrators should take a vow of entrepreneurial chastity, abstaining from the practice of entrepreneurship and investing altogether. Indeed, universities should *want* educators and administrators practicing entrepreneurship and investing. We just don't want them doing it with their own students. That ought not be a surprising dictum; analogs abound. For example,

we want our educators and administrators to develop rich, rewarding, romantic relationships. How wonderful! We just don't want
them doing so with students. Were a professor to make a habit of
dating their students just after graduation, it would surely raise eyebrows. For similar reasons, our eyebrows should stir if someone on
the faculty makes a habit of investing in student ventures.

I know other entrepreneurship educators—good, smart people—
who invest in or otherwise get involved with the ventures of students
(usually on the condition that a student must first graduate). Some
of those faculty can point to gainful profits and grateful students.
But I still don't think they are making the right decision. I file any
profits under what philosophers Bertrand Russel and Thomas Nagel
called "moral luck."[29] If I exceed the speed limit, don't injure any-
body, and profit by getting to my destination faster, it doesn't make
speeding *right* or *moral*. I was just lucky.

Student gratitude is as irrelevant. "Just because the consumer
wishes to enter into a relationship does not mean the professional
should agree." The fiduciary-like responsibilities to students we
have as educators mean we ought to rebuff their overtures for us
to invest and get involved. "When the conflict of interests is great,
the power differential large, and the role expectations incompatible, the potential for harm is so great that the relationships should
be considered a priori unethical."[30]

That is a conclusion I accept reluctantly, although you might not
think so from my arguments here. I *want* to be involved with my students' ventures, which would be fun and profitable. But "the cleanest
solution to handling the potential problems raised by a dual relationship is to avoid it."[31] So, alas, I am stuck on the sideline—a chimera of
coach, cheerleader, and groundskeeper, but not a player in the game.

Accepting my place on the sideline is difficult. I envy the student
founders with whom I work. I want to join them in their adventures. I want to share in their fame. I want to share in their financial returns. Extinguishing these desires required some turning of

my mind. Roman emperor and Stoic philosopher Marcus Aurelius Antoninus wrote, "Take joy and repose in one thing only: to pass from one action accomplished in the service of the community to another action accomplished in the service of the community."[32] *That* is how I now try to think of my role.

Recommendations:

- Entrepreneurship educators should avoid investing in, or becoming involved with, the companies of students and recent graduates. Do not serve on the boards of those companies, consult for them, or otherwise take on roles that conflict with the role of educator.

- IP licensing officers, high-ranking administrators, deans, and department heads have similar powers to those of educators, and therefore ought to eschew investment and involvement in student ventures.

- STEM faculty who cofound companies with students under their supervision should carefully manage their conflicts. One way to do so is to invite an extra faculty member to the student's thesis committee.

4
Educators as Intermediaries

My main duty is teaching classes in entrepreneurship *for credit*. For that reason, I most often see students at the beginning of their entrepreneurship journeys. Many students complete my classes and move on to accelerator programs. Happily, such students usually keep in touch with me and return for my advice.

It was through such advice seeking that years ago, I became aware of a tension between my students and our university's licensing office. Several students visited me simultaneously and complained about the terms of the IP licenses they were offered by the university. These students were each working with faculty innovators on campus on whose research Yale was seeking or had obtained patents. I looked at their draft licenses and concurred that the license terms were not favorable. I suggested the students press their attorneys to negotiate better terms.

It turned out that all of these students had attorneys at the same law firm—one the university had arranged for them to use. Each student told me that they were advised the same thing regarding the licensing agreement: "Just sign it."

I was a bit flummoxed. As a tech entrepreneur, IP scholar, and founder of a patent-related start-up, I knew that the licensing terms were less than awesome. I was surprised these attorneys had not exerted greater effort in pursuit of better terms.

I realized then that a law firm that makes "trouble" for a university is not going to be recommended to that university's student founders. Sitting with these students, I wondered to myself, Who was this firm's *real* client?

I'm not saying that this particular law firm was doing anything untoward. Rather, I'm saying that in our attempt to do a good thing for students—find them legal help—we may have inadvertently created some poor incentives. After all, the university is not apt to recommend a law firm again and again if it is a thorn in its side.

This experience was one of the first that raised my awareness of the nuanced, difficult role educators play as intermediaries between student entrepreneurs and the outside world. In the course of our duties, we introduce students to all manner of people and organizations outside the university, including investors, advisers, well-placed or famous alumni, strategic partners, potential acquirers, customers, accountants, lawyers, and other service providers, such as incubators, coworking facilities, contract research organizations, marketing agencies, regulatory consultants, and software development firms. We are intermediaries connecting student founders to hosts of "outsiders."

Each of these outsiders is important. Entrepreneurship does not happen in a vacuum. Instead, it has a lot of what economists call "agglomeration economies," which is a highfalutin way of saying that entrepreneurship takes a village; it benefits start-ups to be closely located to related start-ups, suppliers, service providers, investors, and customers. Colocated firms benefit from shared resources, matching (e.g., deep markets for labor), and learning through knowledge spillovers.[1] Agglomeration economies are, in short, what make Boston and Silicon Valley such amazing places to be in as a founder: one is surrounded by complements.

Part of my job as a supporter of university entrepreneurship is to bring these complements—these outsiders—into the university so that our student founders can benefit from them. For this reason, one frequently sees investors, lawyers, and outsiders speaking in entrepreneurship classes, judging entrepreneurship competitions, and otherwise roaming around the ivory tower. For many of them, university engagement is a critical form of outreach and a source of potential deals; a law firm sponsors an event on campus instead of supporting some other charitable cause because the sponsorship generates deal flow.

For entrepreneurship educators, the role of intermediary can be precarious. On the one hand, student entrepreneurs benefit from and earnestly desire introductions to service providers, investors, and other complementary outsiders. Educators aid students by providing these introductions, and we most certainly aid students when we help them *avoid* unscrupulous outsiders. On the other hand, the university and its educators have relationships with these outsiders, so we are at risk of making introductions that are self-serving rather than serving the students. For example, I might preferentially introduce the most promising student entrepreneurs to angel investors who are my friends and buddies—thus enriching myself socially or financially. Similarly, I might introduce those promising, profit-prone founders to service providers such as law or accounting firms that sponsor my events on campus or with whom I myself do business. Furthermore, as I described at the start of this chapter, service providers such as attorneys might find themselves overly deferential to the university, which is the source of their deal flow, and therefore less aggressive advocates for individual students.

This chapter is about such conflicts, and it begins with the most fraught intermediation: that between investors and students.

Investors

Entrepreneurship educators, if we are lucky enough to have successful students, will find ourselves introducing those student founders to investors. This is a two-way flow: investors ask for introductions to good student founders and students ask for introductions to good investors. In this chapter, I focus on student introductions to investors. The many issues raised by investors' questions about students, particularly confidentiality, are discussed in chapter 6.

I am one of the aforementioned lucky educators; my students often ask me for introductions to angels, incubators, accelerators, and venture capitalist investors. Given that I know loads of these people, you would think that introductions are always easy and simple. But that is not so.

Consider the many questions. If student founders ask me for an introduction to investors, who should I chose—the "best" or the most famous? I must gauge whether a given student is, in my estimation, ready. If they're great and a "sure bet," do I introduce them to my angel-investing buddies? My friends in venture capital? If a particular venture capital firm sponsored our business plan contest, should I send my student to that firm first?

Surely you see the potential conflicts. It would be quite easy for me to enrich myself—socially and financially, whether in my personal coffers or those of my school—by directing deal flow where it would be beneficial. Conversely, I could suffer socially and financially by not directing deal flow to certain people. After all, it is awkward when a venture capital firm sponsors an event and then learns you didn't send a star founder its way. Ditto for famous donors who are also investors. Deal flow is quite important and valuable to investors.[2] Indeed, the competition for founders is fierce.[3]

As I've already mentioned, an educator's fiduciary-like duties to student founders preclude enriching oneself or one's program at the expense of students. We have a duty to do that which is in students' best interest, which obviously precludes charging students for introductions (see chapter 3) or letting what I'll call "backchannel gains" influence student introductions to investors.

Each of the following situations is an example of a problematic preferential student introduction because it *potentially* results in backchannel gains for educators or the university:

- Introductions to investors who sponsor events at your school
- Introductions to investors in which the university has a financial interest or from which the school receives compensation for referrals
- Introductions to investors in your social network who kiss your ring if you're an educator, invite you to their box seats at the NBA game, pay you as a consultant, or otherwise fawn over you
- Introductions to investors who are donors to the university or powerful alumni
- Introductions to investors who are local and therefore aid local economic development

For example, if I route founders to the venture capital firms that sponsor my school's business plan contest, that is a backchannel gain. I have horse traded and potentially done what is best for me rather than what is best for students.

With so many ways to go wrong, how should educators make introductions? I can only tell you what I do, which is that I strive to *disintermediate* myself. I don't want to be providing introductions. Instead, I strive to create an environment in which investors and students can easily find each other without my help. I haven't quite achieved that, but I'm making progress. Rather than make specific introductions, I keep a list of investors who are alumni of our school, are local, have invested in a previous student, or have expressed an interest to me in investing in our students. When a student asks me for an introduction to an investor, I hand them this list. It's got a few hundred people on it—a decent number of whom come from reputed venture capital firms students instantly recognize.

Students have mixed reactions to this list. They seem pleased to see a nontrivial number of options, but they sometimes appear intimidated by the task that lays before them: reaching out to investors on their own. What students most desire is not a list of self-service options as I provide but rather a personalized, white-glove introduction to a handpicked investor, along with my full-throated endorsement. Well, tough—that's not going to happen for a few reasons. First, by giving (or withholding) an endorsement, I risk betraying confidential information that I acquired through my pedagogical relationships with students (see chapter 3). Second, I simply *cannot* endorse many student start-ups; they're not ventures into which I'd put my own money. Third, I risk the backchannel gains just mentioned. Finally, finding investors on their own is part of an entrepreneur's education; it is a rite of passage and opportunity for growth. I want student founders to do their own homework and find their own investors. Instead of an "arranged marriage," I want them to "fall in love." To the extent I intervene to play the "matchmaker," I am short-circuiting an important part of a founder's development.

Even if I avoid *recommending* particular investors, student founders inevitably ask me questions about them. Students want me to tell them which investors are "good," which are "bad," and what I know. I tell students what I know about investors, but grudgingly and cautiously. I tell students that the *best* source of information about an investor are the student founders with whom the investor worked in the past.

Though I am keen to avoid *recommending* particular investors, I feel I must be a little more forthcoming *warning* about specific ones due to my fiduciary-like duties to students. Let me give you an example. For many years I've invited a delightful, entertaining, and insightful angel investor to school. This person is fabulously wealthy, powerful, and regularly invests in student ventures. But two students I know in whom he invested told me their experiences were not entirely positive. One student even accused the investor of absconding with the student's idea and pursuing it with a different team after a failed negotiation over investment.

I don't know the veracity of these complaints and experiences. Was the investor in the wrong, or were the student founders? It's difficult to be certain (each student was "complicated"). Yet I do not want students to think that by inviting this investor to campus,

I am offering an unequivocal endorsement of him. I have enough of a concern that I now offer student founders a warning about this investor. In so doing, I hope to live by the well-known exhortation of medical ethics: "above all, do no harm."[4]

Attorneys, Accountants, and Other Service Providers

Whereas a founder's relationship with investors is something of a marriage, a founder's relationship with other service providers is more transactional, less permanent, and less dire. It's difficult to get an investor off your cap table—what start-ups use to show ownership stake in the business. It's not so hard to change accountants.

The transactional nature of these relationships makes introductions less sensitive than those to investors. My greatest concern with noninvestor service providers is that they are frequent financial sponsors of on-campus events related to entrepreneurship. For instance, service providers often sponsor business plan contests, giving cash to the university in support of these worthy events as well as discounted services to the student winners. Students are easily misled into thinking that the sponsor of an event—such as a law firm—is the university's *recommendation* to its student founders. But that is not necessarily so.

If the law firm of Dewey, Cheatam, and Howe sponsors a pitch competition on campus, it may be because the firm has a larger marketing budget than rivals or is more desperate for deal flow. It does not mean the firm is students' best choice for legal services, and students should not be led to think as much.

Among the relationships student founders develop with service providers, those with law firms are frequently the most problematic. When universities make legal representation overly easy—such as when students are given free or discounted representation through the sponsor of a school's business plan competition—students can develop an unhealthy dependence on legal counsel and miss the opportunity to understand what kinds of legal tasks they can complete on their own.

Student founders often return to me filled with anxiety after their first meetings with attorneys. They become convinced that every bit of their entrepreneurial activity requires legal counsel and begin to see risks around every corner. Such students can rack up a massive legal tab—a likelihood increased by many law firms' willingness to defer a start-up's bills until series A financing. While it is surely true that entrepreneurship has many risks, it is also true that most start-up legal needs are increasingly doable by oneself, at least in the United States. These include incorporation, trademark and provisional patent filings, and basic contracts such as IP assignments and confidentiality agreements.

My fear of causing legal paranoia and "attorney dependency" in founders was somewhat alleviated in recently years when a few larger, prestigious law firms began to offer self-service "kits" and related material for early stage founders. With such resources at hand, a few short and timely seminars in entrepreneurial law are usually enough to equip founders with a sense of legal confidence, but hopefully not overconfidence. This confidence also helps founders become discerning consumers of legal services, more able to interview law firms and negotiate the terms of their engagement. (US immigration law is an exception, which seems to be so student specific that our school must advise student founders from foreign lands to engage with attorneys quite early in their entrepreneurship journeys.)

Donors and Famous Alumni

Were it not for donors, Yale's growing entrepreneurship program would not exist as it does now. And like many academics, I have a small litany of titles, including an endowed position bearing the name of a generous donor.

Much of academia is like that. It is rare that anything new and wonderful happens at a US school—an effort, program, department, or building—without the generosity and vision of donors, and that has been the case for at least a century. In fact, it was the philanthropy of famous entrepreneurs and businesspeople with last names like Cornell, Hopkins, and Rockefeller that largely funded the emergence of modern US research universities as we know them today in the decades after the Civil War.[5]

The centrality of entrepreneurs among donors is indisputable. Donations to universities set records in each year between 2009 and 2018, rising to $46.7 billion.[6] Modern-day entrepreneurs Bill Gates and Michael Bloomberg are among those who account for gifts in excess of $1 billion each.[7] Entrepreneurship is one of the few ways to make *billions* of dollars, which explains this connection.[8]

My job exists thanks to donors. My office bears the name of a generous donor. My entrepreneurship suite, a gathering place for founders here, bears a donor's name too. Other entrepreneurship spaces on campus have the same, including even multiple *restrooms* at universities named for entrepreneur and investor Brad Feld. One at the University of Colorado at Boulder bears the inscription, "The best ideas come at inconvenient times. Don't ever close your mind to them."[9]

One day, a few years ago, I realized that *my* relationships with donors can get in the way of *students'* relationships with those donors. I was working with our development office on a proposal for a particular donor—an alumnus, luminary, and famous founder—to provide financial support for a series of programs. In the week before I was to make said proposal, a student founder asked me for an introduction to the alumnus donor. As I said before, I try to eschew student requests for introductions to investors, but this was different: the student wanted *advice* from the donor.

Alas, this student was not the best entrepreneur. He had a cock-amamie venture idea, didn't seem to take *my* advice, and hadn't made much progress in the time I had known him. I was disinclined to make the introduction because, to be honest, I was embarrassed by this student. I didn't want the alumnus donor to think he was representative of the other student founders at our school. "These are the kinds of entrepreneurs you're making?" I imagined the alumnus thinking. I also didn't want to waste my precious "social capital" with this donor on a subpar student—potentially putting my proposal at risk.

After some reflection, however, I reversed course, deciding that neither my fear of losing a donation nor this founder's imperfections should stand in the way of the introduction. So instead, I sent one of my first "two-legged" introductions. I emailed the donor and told her the student had asked for an introduction, asked the donor's permission to make the intro, and told the student I had done so. The donor responded to me forthwith, granting her permission, and I introduced the student. I delayed my proposal for the donor, to the chagrin of my development colleagues.

This episode caused me to wonder about how we should factor our personal needs into student requests for introductions to donors and other high-profile persons. I believe I was right to prioritize students' needs over my own and those of my school. Obviously there's a sound consequentialist argument for the opposite conclusion: if I focus on getting donations from donors, or the health of my own personal relationship with famous founders and investors, perhaps the greater good will be served because my entrepreneurship program will thrive. That's a pretty standard tension between consequentialism and deontological/Kantian thinking.

As I emphasized in previous chapters, though, I fall on the Kantian side. I believe my professional, fiduciary-like duty to students—my duty to act in each individual student's best interest—trumps most consequentialist arguments. So I choose to make introductions for students, even when it is inconvenient, or as it often is, embarrassing.

Of course, I want donors and other important stakeholders to see our best and brightest, our most successful founders—the ones who are "crushing it." It's quite likely, however, that my mediocre students need the introductions more than the stars and get more out of those introductions. Moreover, our best students seem less likely to ask for an intro and instead reach out on their own.

What, then, should entrepreneurship educators do? I have met faculty who are covetous and protective of their personal networks either on selfish or consequentialist grounds. For example, I have known faculty to chastise students for contacting, without the faculty's blessing, guests who had visited their classes. How perverse to scold an entrepreneur for being bold! Such students deserve extra credit, not disapprobation. (I discussed educators charging students for introductions to investors in chapter 3. Don't do that.)

I've concluded that I should not "ration" introductions. So I've given up on being a gatekeeper. I make introductions freely, which means I'm sometimes putting mediocre students in touch with famous people I want to impress. I save myself, and them, with the so-called two-legged introduction I described above.

Here's how that works. When a founder asks for an intro to hypothetical Famous Frida, I ask the student a few questions. For example, what does the student know about Famous Frida? I don't insist the students have great answers to these queries, but if they don't, I suggest that it would benefit the student to do a little homework and preparation. Having answered my questions, I ask the student to write an email I can forward to Famous Frida. I preface my forwarded email with a salutation such as, "Frida, this student (below) asked for an intro to you. May I make it?" I don't add judgments, caveats, or endorsements, letting these parties come to know each other without my editorializing.

The two-legged method of introduction has a number of benefits. First, I avoid being a gatekeeper, deciding who is and who isn't worthy of a introduction to donors and other Famous Fridas. Second, Famous Frida has the option to say no or not even reply to my overture. Third, it's easy: having students write their introductions saves me time, and eliminates my risk of erring by inadvertently disclosing confidential information, poorly articulating the founder's activities, failing to offer expected praise, or perjuring myself.

The final benefit is that many ill-prepared founders will simply not take me up on making a two-legged introduction. Such founders are happy to ask for an introduction verbally, but when tasked with writing a brief paragraph, they disappear, poof.

I use two-legged introductions a lot—not just with the Famous Fridas, but even with mundane introductions such as those between fellow students. I eschew the two-legged protocol in two cases: introductions to staff and faculty at my university, and rare introductions with a specific, narrow "ask" by the student founder.

In all of this, I am guided by my underlying belief that student entrepreneurs are—or at least must learn to be—fully capable of representing themselves and their strengths. I am reminded of a story told by Greek Stoic philosopher Epictetus that he attributes to another Greek philosopher, Diogenes:

> Diogenes made an excellent reply to someone who was asking him
> for a letter of recommendation. "That you are a human being,"
> he said, "he'll know as soon as he sees you. Whether you're good or
> bad, he'll know if he's capable of distinguishing good people from
> bad, and if he doesn't know how to do that, ten thousand letters
> from me to him won't make any difference." It's rather as though a
> drachma coin were to ask to be recommended to someone so as to
> be assayed. If the person you want me to write to is a good appraiser,
> you'll recommend yourself.[10]

If my students cannot "recommend themselves," cannot make manifest their own value, what hope for them is there, really? And if the referee, the person to whom my student desires an introduction, cannot discern good founders from bad, well, who would want an introduction to such a person?

Other Students

A few years ago, I worked with a student team making EdTech software that helped teachers with real-time engagement of students in class. Using its app, students could respond to questions, take polls, and play games. The app itself was not rocket science, but the company gained swift traction thanks to a keen understanding of customers and some silver-tongued founders who knew how to sell.

Student founders are at the start of their promising lives and pulled in all directions—by outside job offers, romance, and so on. Some cofounders grow into their roles, becoming amazing entrepreneurs, while others shy away from the experience and their role diminishes. The vacillating roles and fortunes of the company creates a lot of heartache and disagreement, only the veneer of which is visible to entrepreneurship educators.

All of that is generally true, and in this case was exacerbated by the number of students comprising the team. Like many student teams, this one was a bit large in terms of what I've found works best. The potential for conflict scales something like the number of social connections in a small team: two to the power N, where N is the number of cofounders. A team of four or five begins to get weird, and this EdTech student team—which had its share of disputes between its members—had four.

So it was that Bill came to me for advice. He was unhappy with what he felt was cofounder Liam devoting too much time to outside interests. Bill asked me how to get Liam off the team and cap table. As I recall, the company had some verbal agreements about equity and vesting, but nothing had yet been formalized.

Liam had some assets the company needed: relationships with some customers and some software that he had written without an IP assignment. This created a problem.

Without much reflection (cue foreshadowing), I discussed with Bill his options and how to optimize both the outcome for the company and his personal outcome. My advice included both Bill's legal options vis-à-vis Liam and some tactical advice about how he ought to speak to Liam to get what he wanted.

I felt pretty good about my advice, which I thought was solid.

Liam came to see me the next day. He was unhappy with Bill's leadership and uncertain whether he should stay with the team or move to another start-up in a similar space. He wanted my advice on how to make sure he didn't get screwed out of his equity and also whether he'd be able to use the software he had written outside the company.

Crap!

It was only at *that* moment that the obvious dawned on me: Bill and Liam were *both* my students. Neither had more of a claim on me as their teacher than the other, and it was unclear how I ought to counsel them when their needs came into conflict. I decided right then and there that I had to do something that I've never done again, and so I told Liam that Bill had come to see me with similar concerns the day before. I didn't tell Liam the details of my conversation with Bill, but I did tell him that I had given Bill my advice as though I "worked" *solely* for Bill. I promised I would do the same for Liam and would not share our discussion with Bill.

Could such an approach be fair? I'm not sure it was.

The episode raises a host of ethical questions for educators. When students are in dispute, to whom is our allegiance? Is it to the company, CEO, each student equally, or some combination? If one student is in my class and another is not, or one student is in my department and another is not, that would seem to be problematic too. Occasionally, a student's cofounder is not a student at all but still regularly meets with me in the context of the team's studies at Yale. How does that get handled? And what if one student is a founder and the other an intern?

Like most entrepreneurship educators, I've seen a great many internecine disputes between students working on start-ups. These are a leading cause of start-up failure.[11] Since my experience with Liam and Bill, I watch for brewing disputes and take care to avoid being overly involved. My role is to teach students how to resolve their own disputes. It is not to resolve the disputes for them, and it is *certainly not* to use my power over the students to resolve the dispute—for example, to dictate who is right or wrong, who should get what equity, or who should play what role. Each of those is for students to decide among themselves. My role is to educate them so they can do so.

Companies

If I had a dime for every time I've heard from an alumnus looking for an MBA student to help them out with a business, I would have a *lot* of dimes. Stakeholders in the broad entrepreneurship ecosystem— typically alumni, local businesspersons, and even faculty—frequently ask for my help finding students to aid them in some effort. The canonical version is from an alumnus who is starting a new business and wants an MBA student to create a business plan or do marketing research.

These are rarely compensated opportunities. Instead, the stakeholders say that students will benefit from the *experience* they'll gain, exposure to an industry, or the expansion of their networks. Quite often, the inquirer wants free labor; in lieu of compensation, the inquirer wants me to offer students course credit. Doing so would be easy. I could offer a practicum, for credit, in which students work for alumni ventures or local start-ups. But to do so would be ethically dubious.

There are at least a few risks. One is that many student entrepreneurs are, in general (and not just if they're in one of my classes), inclined to do whatever I ask of them. They understand that I hold the key to many of the university's resources, and am able to bring that to bear in support of their ventures and their careers. That kind of "power" is potentially problematic in and of itself.

Add to this that I don't want to use these powers to compel students to do work that benefits *me*. Farming out my students would be an easy way to enrich myself socially. Every entrepreneurship educator likely has the potential for this ethical problem, especially since many of those come asking for students to "work" for them without compensation will be entrepreneurs with whom we have close relationships. And what if the entrepreneur making the request is a university donor, famous, or powerful in some other way—alumnus or not?

Even offering course credit is ethically problematic. Does *any* work for a start-up have educational benefit for a student? I'm not certain it is always the same as taking a class, but where is the line between something worth and not worth credit? And making all of this even more problematic, the students might be asked to sign NDAs or IP assignment agreements as a condition of their participation (see chapter 6).

All of these ethical risks are related to my professional obligations to students and possibly also my obligations, in a Kantian sense, not to use students as a mere means to an end. This is why I *never* arrange such internships.

Is there an alternative? At Yale, I can point the person making the request to a variety of resources on campus that could help them find students on their own (ranging from student clubs to the career development office), without my recommendation of individuals or any pressure from me on those students. I usually tell the inquirer that I am also not a great way to find students. What fraction of our student body do I see? A small one. Our career development office sees many more. Moreover, an open solicitation in a club reaches numerous students. Those are better mechanisms and less ethically problematic.

Practitioners

As Bennis and O'Toole observed in the *Harvard Business Review*, "Today it is possible to find tenured professors of management who have never set foot inside a real business, except as customers," and "one unfortunate result of this trend has been that many B schools have to hire adjunct professors to teach required MBA courses."[12]

I am not sure I would call this situation "unfortunate" so much as necessary to the extent that we feel practitioners—adjunct professors in the foregoing—can impart something we wish imparted to students, but that the full-time faculty cannot themselves provide. More than in other areas of study, we have some sense in entrepreneurship that theory is insufficient: it alone cannot make our students into good entrepreneurs. In addition to grasping theory, we want our students to develop "know-how," a practical capacity to excel in the craft of entrepreneurship.[13]

Alas, imparting know-how to students can be a difficult task for research-focused faculty, who lack—or at least have not demonstrated in their lives—the practical capacity to excel in entrepreneurship. As Aristotle observed in his *Nicomachean Ethics*, know-how is learned through *practice*, though doing. "We learn an art or craft by doing the things that we shall have to do when we have learnt it: for instance, men become builders by building houses, harpers by playing on the harp."[14]

The importance of practice in entrepreneurship education means that a role, some role, for practitioners is helpful. So more often than in most other disciplines, entrepreneurship educators invite practitioners into the university as speakers, mentors, judges, and adjunct faculty as well as to play other part-time educator roles. This makes entrepreneurship like the arts, drama, and creative writing— disciplines that put a premium on practice and in which practitioners are commonplace.

The benefits of involving these practitioners, though, come with complications. The first is that these practitioners bring with them the ethical norms of the *marketplace*, which frequently conflict with the ethical norms of academia. I'm not saying practitioners are *unethical*. Indeed, most practitioners who contribute to students' education are fantastic, caring, generous people. It's just that they can be unaware of their ethical obligations vis-à-vis students of the sort this book addresses.

Let me give you an example. I once had a practitioner teach a class related to consumer web applications. They had great practical knowledge and experience around customer discovery and low-code prototyping. One day, they told me about meeting with student founder who had a venture in the practitioner's market—in fact, one quite similar to the practitioner's own venture, which I'll call FuzzCo.

This practitioner told me that the student had asked her about FuzzCo's market size, customers, and business strategy, and she suspected the student was digging for competitive, proprietary information. She bragged to me that she gave the student "bullshit answers."

Apoplectic, I told her that under no circumstances, ought one give students bullshit answers. Sure, that might be morally permissible in the marketplace, where many think "it should be universally understood and expected that those who ask questions which they have no right to ask will have lies told to them."[15] But lies and bullshit are anathema to educators' pedagogical duty. This practitioner, feeling inappropriately questioned, instead ought to have demurred and declined to answer our student's inquiries.

To be clear, I tell practitioners about their obligations to students and the norms of academia. So do most entrepreneurship educators I know. Indeed, some universities even do background checks on practitioners, while others ask practitioners, such as mentors participating in university accelerators, to agree in writing to eschew investment in student ventures during their formal involvement on campus. But such agreements are not a panacea; not all universities use them, and in any case they are, at best, an "incomplete contract."[16] What I want from practitioners is not strict adherence to a set of rules but rather an attitude, good judgment, and a faculty-like orientation toward my students. I wish for them to view students as I do.

I cannot contract for that—and so like many faculty, I don't. I tend to find practitioners through experiment, through numerous small, positive interactions that help me be certain a practitioner threads the needle I need threaded. I invite a practitioner to an extracurricular event, and if it goes well, maybe I invite them to meet with students and hold office hours. If that goes well, maybe they give a talk on campus. Maybe they teach an extracurricular short course. Maybe they are a mentor to students. If all goes well, maybe they teach their own course. It's not an efficient process. I see many faculty doing the same. This is, I think, why "good" practitioners persist so long in universities: they are precious and hard to find.

When things go bad, it's potentially devastating for students and a painful mess for everyone else. The most well-known case of this involved investor and entrepreneur Joe Lonsdale, himself well-known as the billionaire founder of the analytics firm Palantir. Lonsdale reportedly entered into a romantic relationship with a student "while he was her assigned mentor for an undergraduate course at Stanford called Technology Entrepreneurship."[17]

The university determined that "Lonsdale violated Stanford Admin Guide Policy 1.7.2, which bans sexual and romantic relationships between teachers, including mentors, and undergraduate students," and "banned him from mentoring undergraduates for

10 years."[18] It should be noted that the university initially banned Lonsdale from campus entirely for ten years, but reversed course when evidence indicated his relationship with the student was consensual.[19]

Thankfully, such situations are rare. I have seen or know of other ethical violations: mentors not keeping student information confidential; mentors who personally committed not to invest in students still investing surreptitiously through friends and family; mentors pressuring students for board seats or consulting arrangements; mentors attempting to supplant student founders in a venture; and mentors just generally being untrustworthy. These thankfully are rare too.

The most common failing of mentors is more mundane: a good number are just useless to students. The archetype of a less-than-useful mentor is the well-meaning but entirely overconfident twenty-year veteran of corporate America who finds himself in the mentoring corps of his local college or alma mater, living vicariously through young founders. Such a mentor lacks both the theoretical understanding of the professorate *and* practical wisdom acquired through the lived experience of entrepreneurship. He is, therefore, a potentially dangerous armchair quarterback. And when not dangerous, they're mostly useless. In my experience, truly experienced founders and investors are intuitively safer bets.

Alas, it is difficult to find truly experienced founders and investors willing to be involved in one's university (much less those who are good at mentoring and teaching). There is, to some extent, an adverse selection problem.[20] Those whom I wish to be mentors, be involved in courses, or teach a course have the least time, are the most hesitant, and require the most convincing. In contrast, I am inundated with inquiries from practitioners I wouldn't let near students. These are people who have no experience teaching and yet ardently wish to share their anecdotal experiences with students. Many desire the credentialing and prestige of a university affiliation. They are "in it" for the wrong reasons and "wrong for it" to begin with. Filtering out such practitioners—telling them no—is laborious, uncomfortable, and ultimately insufficient.

Even experienced founders and investors with impeccable bona fides and selfless motivations are not necessarily good mentors or instructors. Many practitioners imagine they can parachute into the classroom and casually drop wisdom on rapt, would-be acolytes. It is not so. Teaching is a challenging, nuanced, emotional labor that requires practice and tends to consume all the oxygen in one's life.[21] Many practitioners "fail" in teaching when confronted with the throngs of needy students and their ineluctable, inbox-filling demands. In short, teaching *well* is not something one does easily part time and thus is a problem for practitioners.

Finally, it is unclear that what practitioners teach is what the university wishes to be taught. Generally speaking, universities want students to be taught what we *know* about entrepreneurship: that which is supported by empirical research and sound theory. We do not wish our classrooms to look like the business schools of yore, "more akin to trade schools" in which "most professors were good ole boys dispensing war stories, cracker-barrel wisdom, and the occasional practical pointer."[22]

Students are done a disservice and potentially imperiled when they take anecdote as truth, generalizing from the bespoke experiences of the war storyteller. "Business educators have always faced the dilemma of academic rigor pitted against practical relevance."[23] Practitioners provide *relevance*, which is wonderful, but in so doing we ought not sacrifice *rigor*. The struggle is to find a sweet spot, an acceptable compromise between the two.

In short, like so many other entrepreneurship educators, I often bring practitioners into our university to share their expertise, mentor, lecture, and teach classes. The practitioners bring great benefit to students, yes. But there is also the potential for harm whenever educators act as intermediaries, connecting students to the outside world. Students can easily presume that outsiders—practitioners we invite into the classroom, law firms that sponsor pitch competitions, or investors to whom we introduce student founders—are bound by the same rules as educators; that outsiders have students' best interests at heart and are just like faculty.

They are not, however, and nor should they be. These outsiders have their own interests, moral obligations, priorities, and expertise—different than educators. That is a *good* thing. Their differences are why we invite them in. They have, in the case of practitioner founders, done the deed and can tell students firsthand how theory is manifest in practice. They have something special to offer our students. The trick is to gain what benefit is to be had and minimize the risk of harm.

Recommendations:

- Educators should strive to disintermediate themselves so as to create an environment in which student founders and service providers such as investors, attorneys, and accountants can easily find each other.

- Educators should make introductions that are in the best interest of student founders and be weary of backchannel gains. For example, educators ought not preferentially send founders to investors who sponsor on-campus events or are powerful university alums.

- Educators should help students become discerning consumers of service providers, particularly legal service providers, and have them procure these services on their own. Arranging such services for students can dampen students' development, and in some cases, create a dependency in which student founders do not understand what they are capable of doing for themselves.

- Educators should make sure students know that service providers who visit campus or sponsor events on campus are not necessarily the preferred or recommended providers of the university.

- Avoid injecting yourself into student disputes. Students should solve disputes themselves. Remember that an educator's obligations are to students individually and equally, not to the start-up.

- Be wary of offering course credit to students working for outside companies. Such students should be paid for their labors. And those experiences rarely have the pedagogical potential companies claim; it's frequently just work nobody at the company wants to do.

- It's difficult to find practitioners who can put themselves in the shoes of educators, and especially those who can teach in a way that blends both practice (relevance) and theory (rigor). Use numerous, small interactions to find practitioners who can do so.

5
Problematic Student Start-ups

When a student from our divinity school enrolled in my introductory entrepreneurship class, we met to ensure their proposed project satisfied the requirements specified in my syllabus. Projects should be tractable and amenable to an evidence-based approach. Student entrepreneurs should talk to customers, create prototypes of their products, and generally approach their ventures as scientists.

She described her project to me. "I want to create a sex robot."

"OK," I said. "How do you mean, exactly?"

"Like a robot that has sex with you."

"Please open my door," I responded.

Let me mention that the mission of the Yale Divinity School is "to foster the knowledge and love of God through scholarly engagement with Christian traditions in a global, multifaith context."[1] As you might imagine, this was an unusual venture for a divinity student. It was even unusual and awkward for me. I was not enthused to discuss sex robot prototyping and customer development with this student; I certainly wasn't going to do it without witnesses and hence the door opening.

I tell you this sex robot story mostly because I find it funny, particularly because the idea came from a divinity school student. I don't think this student's venture presented many ethical problems. That's not to say there are *zero* ethical problems with sex robots. For example, entrepreneurship educators in religious universities might find sex robots unethical (I don't know). Further, we might worry that sex robots have deleterious effects on their users or society. And we might even worry about outlandish dystopian outcomes akin to HBO's *Westworld* series in which sentient robots are subject to sexual assault and other horrors.

I wasn't worried about those things. I'm pretty much fine with the ethics of a sex robot venture. Having said that, I *still* didn't want that venture in my class for purely selfish reasons: supporting student ventures like that is potentially embarrassing and a pain in the neck. For instance, I cringe imaging my faculty colleagues reading an article in the student newspaper describing my mentorship of the Robo Pleasure Bot 5000 venture.

The sex robot venture was a *problematic* venture—for one of the many reasons ventures might fall into this category. This one was *embarrassing*. Other ventures might be problematic because they are illegal, unethical, or just plain bad businesses. Should entrepreneurship educators support problematic ventures? Do we have an obligation to do so? Is it OK to discriminate against these ventures? If we support a problematic one, ought its founders receive the same attention from the university as other students?

In this chapter, I describe problematic ventures that prompt such questions and offer some answers. I begin not with the scandalous or illegal but rather the banal: ventures that are just bad.

Bad Ventures

I wish I could say that students at my august Ivy League institution create only great ventures. Alas, it is not so. A large percentage of the students I see—some of the smartest students in the world,

I believe—have dreadful start-up ideas. What makes them dreadful? Consider the well-known characteristics of "good" ventures: a large and growing market, experienced team, sustainable competitive advantage, customers with a well-understood problem or "pain," and so on.[2] Now think about ventures that have none of these things. Plenty of student ventures are like *that*.

Like many faculty, I find bad ventures problematic. I wonder whether I should turn students with bad ventures away at my door or have some duty to help students improve their bad ventures. Is my time better spent on "good" ventures? If I work with bad ones, will the student founders think I'm endorsing their ventures? Do I risk creating future "zombie ventures"—bad ventures kept alive that would have otherwise died a natural death? These are difficult questions. I'm not certain of their answers; as I discuss below, however, I think the balance of argument suggests that I have some duty to work with bad ventures and that doing so can have good consequences.

Consider the following hypothetical but realistic situation in which I need to choose between two founders. Awesome Alice and Bad Bob are vying for the last spot in an entrepreneurship class. As her name implies, Alice has an awesome venture, and Bob not so much. Imagine all else is equal—for instance, Alice and Bob are just as smart and hardworking. Should I admit Alice or Bob to the class? I don't believe that a Kantian analysis has much to offer here. Kant would say I have obligations to these students and promises to keep due to my relationships with them, but nothing about distinguishing between the students. And I think my professional duty to each Alice and Bob, by virtue of my teacher-student relationship, is equal.

So who do I admit to the class? I believe the *typical* answer is meritocratic: *Alice* ought to be admitted. Indeed, for years I admitted the Awesome Alices to my entrepreneurship classes and refused the Bad Bobs. But I came to doubt the wisdom of that approach, relying not on Kant, who doesn't tell me much here, but on the consequentialists Mill and Bentham. I came to believe that educating the Bad Bobs can have better consequences.

In a famous study at Harvard, Josh Lerner and Ulrike Malmendier showed that MBA students randomly assigned into a group of peers enriched for entrepreneurs had better outcomes: groups with experienced founders created start-ups that on average, lived longer, were better funded, and enjoyed greater success.[3] This success, though, was not because mediocre would-be entrepreneurs got *better*; rather, it was because crummy would-be entrepreneurs elected not to pursue their *bad* ideas, thus raising the average amount of success.

I find this study delightful because it points out something we don't often think about as entrepreneurship educators. We tend to focus on the best founders, but a vital good we provide through teaching is *fixing* the bad ventures and even *dissuading* people from entrepreneurship. Woe be to the Bad Bob pursuing a doomed venture on graduation. How wonderful to not turn Bad Bob away but instead, through education, help him understand *why* his venture is bad and *how* to build a better one. A student dissuaded from a bad venture can pivot to a better one or choose another career altogether, perhaps returning to entrepreneurship later, finding themselves thankful for the skill set to critically evaluate and fix bad ventures.

All too often, students and faculty alike buy into the myth that college is the best time to start a venture, that entrepreneurship is a game for the ramen-eating, hoodie-wearing young. While the venture that students found or work on in class is typically their first, it is rarely their last. They have an entire lifetime in front of them in which to be entrepreneurial. In fact, research shows that the median founder age of the fastest-growing firms in the United States is around forty-five.[4] And founders with industry expertise—adults with work experience, networks, and access to capital—are more likely to be successful.

By that consequentialist logic, I have come to believe that when I'm forced to choose between educating an Awesome Alice or a

Bad Bob, Bob is not such a bad choice. Just as a doctor sees the sick before the healthy, prioritizing the Bobs can achieve much good. I don't have to worry so much about Awesome Alice. She can look after herself and is already on the right track; it's Bad Bob who needs educating. Bad Bob has more to learn.

I want to be clear that I'm talking *education* and not *acceleration*. I'm talking about the ordinary pedagogical resources here of the sort described in chapter 2. If there's an *award* for entrepreneurship, such as a small amount of grant funding or admission to an extracurricular accelerator, clearly Awesome Alice deserves the award and not Bad Bob. To give Bob the award is perverse and creates a *moral hazard*: it subsidizes and endorses a bad venture. (Avoiding endorsement of bad ventures is a major component of the next section, "Lifestyle Ventures.") But if a resource is *pedagogical*—that is, we're *educating* entrepreneurs—I think there's a strong consequentialist argument that educating Bob produces superior outcomes to educating Alice.

There's also an ancillary point to make: educating Bad Bob is likely easier. Alice, being awesome, is probably further along in her venture and in need of bespoke guidance related to her market, customers, investors, and such. Bad Bob just needs the basics. I could educate five Bobs in the time it would take to help Alice. And Alice, due to her awesomeness, surely has access to many mentors other than our faculty.

I don't want to make too much of this assertion. It's enough to know that Awesome Alice does not *prima facie* merit educators' attention more than Bad Bob. One can accomplish much good dissuading the delusional rather than accelerating the awesome. Alas, working with the Bad Bobs of the world is less fun than working with the Awesome Alices—which I think is one reason that many educators focus on the Alices versus the Bobs. Moreover, I think many educators confuse contexts in which they should be educating with those for accelerating, with the latter being almost exclusively extracurricular (unless you teach in a vocational school).

While I think working with Bad Bobs is good and right, it can be awkward. From time to time, a colleague will accost me on campus, wanting to speak about a student entrepreneur. "I spoke to Bob," my colleague might say, "the student in your class doing on-campus drone sandwich delivery. That's a terrible business!"

"Yes, I know." It's the only reply I have, and it's a sheepish one. "He'll come around to that realization too."

Like most entrepreneurship educators, my resources are finite, and so I must compromise between serving the Awesome Alices and Bad Bobs. Every year, I find myself denying students entrance to our capstone Start-up Founder Practicum because they are "too advanced." A few years ago, a student applied who had created a line of Bluetooth headphones. This was before such devices were ubiquitous; this student's was one of the few brands on the market, and it was stocked by a major retailer with stores across the United States. He was flummoxed when I denied him entry to the class. Yet the truth was that he already knew most of what he would have been taught in the class. He had access to mentors and investors outside class too. In his place, I could admit a student who would benefit more from our faculty, whose time was limited.

If I had been running an accelerator or extracurricular program, I would have admitted that student in a heartbeat. He was a great founder. But I was teaching a class, the purpose of which was education. This student was such an Awesome Alice that my marginal contribution to his education and venture would have been de minimis. (Alas, I'm certain that if he makes it rich as a founder, and Yale's development office comes calling, I've ruined any chance for our university to benefit from this alum's philanthropy.)

Though the Bad Bobs in my life are problematic, I think the balance of argument suggests that I ought to admit some of them to entrepreneurship classes and workshops, and generally permit students with bad ventures to avail themselves of my university's routinely offered pedagogical resources without discrimination as opposed to dismissing the Bad Bobs out of hand.

Lifestyle Ventures

One kind of "bad" venture is particularly common among would-be student entrepreneurs: the lifestyle venture. In entrepreneurship parlance, we use that characterization for just about anything that isn't a high-growth, scalable, venture-capital-backable company. For instance, some of my students started a fast-casual Italian restaurant. A married student couple started a brewery-bar combo. Every year, I see students wishing to start consultancies or artisanal food businesses. These are all lifestyle ventures: they lack the potential for high growth, venture capitalists are not going to fund them, and the founders cannot expect an initial public offering or acquisition windfall. These ventures are bad in the sense that they are not scalable and are in competitive, stagnant markets with low barriers to entry along with few opportunities for liquidity.

At "top-tier" universities, students starting lifestyle ventures often receive little support. Some educators don't even think the founders of lifestyle ventures are entrepreneurs—and those educators are not entirely wrong. The founders of lifestyle ventures bear scant resemblance to the classic, Schumpeterian entrepreneur.[5] To Schumpeter, the famous economist of innovation, "the entrepreneur is the disruptive force that dislodges the market from the somnolence of equilibrium."[6] Indeed, that is not an apt description of a student starting a fast-casual Italian restaurant. Moreover, lifestyle ventures do not produce the job growth, local economic development, and—let's be honest—headlines, school rankings, and wealthy alumni that universities crave.[7]

Despite these shortcomings, I tend to admit the founders of lifestyle ventures into our entrepreneurship courses and support them alongside other entrepreneurs for a few reasons. First, my view of entrepreneurship is rather broad. Imagine a spectrum of humankind. On the one hand, we have corporate plebeians punching the clock who are categorically not entrepreneurial, and and on the other hand, we have Richard Branson and his ilk. Between those two extremes is an array of professional behaviors that *look* entrepreneurial: "intra-preneurship," side hustles, and start-ups of various character. I do not know where to draw the line and call one person an entrepreneur and the person to their left not an entrepreneur. I suspect I am more inclusive than most entrepreneurship faculty. I *do* know that students starting lifestyle ventures are *starting something* and have much to gain from our entrepreneurship classes (even if educating those founders doesn't produce a bunch of benefits for the university).

The second reason I permit lifestyle ventures in my entrepreneur-ship classes is that I feel I must meet students impartially *where they are*. The students of mine who wanted to start a brewery had a passion. They were graduating from our MBA program and not looking for other jobs. They had burned the proverbial ships and were "all-in" on their lifestyle venture. I feel that these students are just as worthy of my support as the student starting "the next Facebook." Many students from my university also choose to become artists, actors, and scholars of ancient Sanskrit. Like starting a restaurant, each of those is an unremunerative choice. They are not the choices for me, but "to each their own."

My most important task when working with lifestyle entrepreneurs in class is to avoid the moral hazard that would be created by *endorsing* their business. I do not wish them to leave my class thinking that because they worked on their idea with me, I think their idea is good. I make sure that the student founders of lifestyle ventures know what awaits them: they will work harder than other founders with fewer resources and for less return. Their lifestyle venture could eat a decade of their life and leave them little to show for it. That being said, we know that entrepreneurship has substantial nonpecuniary benefits that are, I believe, just as available to lifestyle entrepreneurs as other entrepreneurs (see chapters 1 and 7). These benefits include being your own boss, choosing your own schedule, living where you wish, working with whom you choose, and most important, living a grand adventure.

Still, in many ways, lifestyle entrepreneurs have bad ventures. I insist that they acknowledge this as a condition of working with them in class. I try to achieve something like the informed consent I discussed in chapter 2 on university investments. If students demonstrate that they understand the downsides of their lifestyle ventures and *still* wish to proceed, I will treat them like any other student entrepreneur. I tolerate no ambiguity; I sometimes even ask students to acknowledge the downsides of their ventures *in writing*. After that, I pledge not to bring it up again. I agree to move forward with the student's idea, *without* my continual disapprobation.

Illegal Ventures

In HBO's *The Wire*, heroin dealer Stringer Bell, fresh off recent management training, convenes collaborators to discuss a new business plan. His assistant dutifully takes notes, for which Mr. Bell chastises him: "Is you taking notes on a criminal fucking conspiracy?" I have, on the occasion of meeting with certain students, indeed felt as if I was taking notes on a criminal conspiracy.

I don't mean that students propose to me ventures that are *obviously* illegal, like Assassins-for-Hire.com. But with fair frequency, students work on legally questionable ventures—that is, those in which the entrepreneurs *might* be breaking the law (somewhere) or inducing others to do so. I find these ventures problematic.

The most common legal transgressions are banal. Students starting a food-related business are likely violating local food preparation laws and health codes; there's a reason restaurants are licensed and you can't just sell cookies out of your car.[8] International students who found companies likely violate the terms of their visa in the United States or United Kingdom.[9] The rules are more permissive in some EU countries. Students working on cannabis ventures are often in violation of US federal law.[10]

Such legal transgressions are not exclusive to hapless student entrepreneurs. Indeed, start-ups flouting the law are often in the news.
Uber operated in localities where it was illegal and developed software
to evade detection by law enforcement.[11] Airbnb was fined for violating housing regulations that prohibit short-term rentals.[12] Thousands
of start-ups skirted securities laws through "initial coin offerings."[13]
To the extent that "move fast and break things" is the battle cry of the
start-up world, it seems that *laws* are frequently the things broken.

Are start-ups that break the law doing anything unethical? Legality and ethics are related, but distinct concepts; "illegal ventures," by
which I mean start-ups breaking the law, are not necessarily "unethical
ventures." Although that which is illegal is often unethical—murder,
assault, theft, and so on—some laws have no ethical connotation
whatsoever; in the United Kingdom, for instance, the law stipulates
that one must drive on the left side of a road, whereas in the United
States it is on the right side. And in some cases, laws themselves are
unethical. Segregation and gender-related laws in the United States
prohibited ordinary moral behavior for much of US history: voting,
marrying the partner of your choice, and participating in the workplace without discrimination. To this day, domestic abuse—clearly
an unethical behavior—is legal in some of the world's countries.[14]

Take the case of Yale University occasionally hosting a Business
of Cannabis conference. Many Yale student entrepreneurs are interested in cannabis, and some of the most successful entrepreneurs in
the cannabis industry are Yale alumni.[15] Cannabis, though, is *illegal*
at a federal level in the United States as I write this; like heroin,
cannabis is a Schedule I substance under the federal Controlled
Substance Act, meaning "it has a high potential for abuse and no
acceptable medicinal use."[16] (I recognize that this cannabis example
might seem quaint in the near future given that cannabis's status as
a Schedule I substance is more a product of politics than science.[17]
But today it has the potential to put a university's federal funding
at risk, which is why some universities prohibit their faculty from

supporting students working on cannabis ventures.) Perhaps Yale is hosting a conference of cannabis criminals. Yet few people, I suspect, would say those founders are doing anything unethical.

So am I "OK" supporting student cannabis ventures? And more generally, if legality and ethics are distinct, ought we entrepreneurship educators to support student founders who flout the law? That is a complicated question, in large part because not all laws are equal. In his "Letter from a Birmingham Jail," US civil rights leader Martin Luther King Jr. wrote,

> One may well ask: "How can you advocate breaking some laws and obeying others?" The answer lies in the fact that there are two types of laws: just and unjust. I would be the first to advocate obeying just laws. One has not only a legal but a moral responsibility to obey just laws. Conversely, one has a moral responsibility to disobey unjust laws. I would agree with St. Augustine that "an unjust law is no law at all."[18]

King went on to describe unjust laws as those in conflict with "moral," "natural," and "eternal" law, echoing Augustine.

Few start-ups flouting the law have King's moral high ground. He was imprisoned for trumped-up offenses such as "parading without a permit" in his noble effort to end US segregation. Compare his fight with Uber's against regulations disadvantageous to its business—a process that included the company identifying users likely to be law enforcement officials and purposefully evading those officials by using "ghost cars" and other techniques.[19] It wasn't exactly a courageous act of civil disobedience.

Some laws benefit us, whereas others might be a pain; in sum, though, they increase our collective welfare. Unless you have a cause as worthy as King's, a moral person ought not pick and choose which laws to follow. This was vividly illustrated in Plato's *Crito*, wherein Socrates was convicted of corrupting the youths of Athens and sentenced to death by poison. His friends arranged an escape, but Socrates demurred, posing the rhetorical question, "Do you imagine that a city can continue to exist and not be turned upside down, if the legal judgments which are pronounced in it have no force but are nullified and destroyed by private persons?"[20]

Then Socrates imagined his fellow Athenians asking him, "What charge do you bring against us and the state, that you are trying to destroy us? Did we not give you life in the first place? Was it not through us that your father married your mother and begot you? Tell us, have you any complaint against those of our laws that deal with marriage?"[21]

Socrates's point is that he benefited from the laws of Athens throughout his life. Indeed, he exists *because* of those laws. By what right and logic would he trample on the laws now? In a similar fashion, in the United States it is our laws and institutions that allow entrepreneurs to thrive. How many start-ups would exist without contract, corporate, and IP laws? Just as a mighty oak takes root and grows where soil is fertile, so too do great start-ups flourish where the laws protect and encourage them.[22] By what right and logic would a founder discard the law when they find it inconvenient? To do so would be hypocritical and give license to our fellow citizens who wish to ignore laws that *they* deem inconvenient.

This line of thought is called "social contract theory," or "contractarianism," and was the major intellectual contribution of philosopher Thomas Hobbes.[23] He thought that through our tacit acquiescence to a set of laws, collective welfare is improved, we become individually protected from the abuse of others, and benefit from the cooperation of others.[24] This social contract is, in Hobbes's view, what rescues humanity from a life that is otherwise "nasty, brutish, and short."[25]

May entrepreneurs advocate to change laws? Surely. Should they violate the law? Generally, no. We educators should be circumspect supporting students who might run afoul of the law. If we expect that a student entrepreneur may do so, we have a fiduciary-like duty to ensure the student understands our concern so that we might prevent them from rushing headlong into legal peril. Does a student founder understand that their cannabis venture might expose them to legal peril? Do they understand that working on their venture might violate the terms of their immigration status? Do they understand they might be skirting labor laws by employing people as contractors? Do they understand what manner of investment solicitations are permitted by securities law? As educators, we ought to ask ourselves and students such questions. (Again, this is similar to the concept of informed consent discussed in chapter 2.)[26]

In addition to our obligations to students and our duty ourselves to follow the law as moral citizens, we educators have duties to our universities. I have a duty not to embroil Yale in illegal activity and thereby imperil the other good work of the university. I look at these educator-university obligations later in this chapter.

Embarrassing Ventures

Some ventures are problematic not because they're bad or illegal businesses but merely because they're embarrassing for entrepreneurship educators. For example, I find student sex-related ventures, like the robot sex venture I described at this chapter's start, pretty embarrassing. These are not the kinds of ventures schools are touting on social media or featuring in their alumni magazines.

I often worry that I am unjustly biased against the founders of embarrassing ventures, and that as a result, these founders do not receive the same education or support from our institution as other founders do. The university has tremendous resources; as its agent, I can bring those resources to bear in support of student founders. I admit certain students—and not others—to a class, program, or fellowship. I give ventures office space. I invite student founders to meet with donors, investors, and illustrious guests. I even purchase the products of student founders. For instance, most years, I buy a selection of goods from our student entrepreneurs who make consumer products and then send those products in gift boxes to donors so that the donors may experience firsthand the wonderful work of Yale's student founders. Last year, I sent donors a gift box of student-crafted soap, tequila, charcuterie, and other goodies.

One year, a student named Sarah was in my entrepreneurship class. Her venture made sex toys with female empowerment branding—dildos, vibrators, and other carnal delights sold direct to consumers. I never sent any of Sarah's products to my donors, even though Sarah was a talented founder making great progress on her venture and I believed in her mission. Was Sarah any less worthy of my support than the students making soap?

If a gift basket seems like low stakes, consider another example. Years ago, two founders in my class ran a crowdfunding campaign for their venture, which sold sustainably produced business wear. Multiple departments at our school used their departments' social media clout to drive would-be donors to the student's crowdfunding campaign, which became a great success. I doubt Yale would have done the same for Sarah's sex toy venture, for the same reasons I excluded her products from my donor gift basket: embarrassment and perhaps a hint of puritanical prejudice.

In retrospect, I regret my decision. I should have treated Sarah like any other founder. I should have sent the dildos to my donors.

Since my experience with Sarah, I try to treat the founders of embarrassing ventures the same as other founders. I don't always succeed. A few years ago, Matt—a soft-spoken student involved in many social justice causes on campus—applied to one of our for-credit entrepreneurship classes. He wanted to start a pornography venture.

"Real porn?" I asked.

Yes, Matt told me, *real* porn: people having sex on video. But Matt wanted to make what he called "ethical porn." He would respect sex workers' desires, pay workers a living wage, and tend to workers' health, both mental and physical. Matt even had market research suggesting that consumers of porn would pay a premium to know it was made "ethically."

I hesitated to admit Matt to my class. In particular, I worried about the reactions of my colleagues and donors—I suspected they wouldn't be jazzed to hear about me helping a student make porn. At the same time, I knew Matt was not proposing to do anything *illegal*. Indeed, porn is *legal* in the United States, and many people make a fine business of it. I worried that I was discriminating against Matt's porn venture in the same way I had discriminated against Sarah's sex toy venture. I wanted to treat Matt fairly and impartially to avoid secretly judging his venture as I had done with Sarah's. But I also had the sense that maybe Matt's venture was potentially not just embarrassing for me. Maybe it was also potentially embarrassing for my school. I felt I had a duty to inform Yale and did so by describing my predicament to senior colleagues. (For a more thorough discussion, see the next section, "Obligations to the University.")

After speaking with my colleagues, we concluded that allowing Matt in my class could have undesirable consequences for Yale and potentially his classmates, some of whom had already complained to me about his venture. Most of those complaining felt that ethical porn was an oxymoron: any kind of porn was exploitive and unethical. (I talk about unethical ventures later in this chapter. I didn't feel Matt's venture was unethical; it seemed to me that he was trying to *improve* the ethics of the pornography industry. But I understood others felt differently.)

Ultimately, I decided on a compromise. I denied Matt admission to the class, offering instead to do an independent study with him alone, for which I would not receive teaching credit. In that way, the possible negative fallout from Matt's embarrassing venture was more "on me" and marginally less on the school. Further, Matt's schoolmates would not be challenged with his presence daily.

Matt's venture never took off. Within a few months, he had pivoted to something less controversial, and I ended up admitting him to the class in the next term. I never felt good about my compromise. I worried that I had denied Matt the company of his peers and a rich, cohort-based learning environment in order to save myself embarrassment. Maybe if I had the stomach for a few uncomfortable conversations, I could have served him better.

Although it sounds stupid to say so, I often think about how I treated Sarah and Matt. I found my experiences with those students interesting because it wasn't clear to me what the *right thing* to do was. On the one hand, I feel that perhaps I have the unchecked right to support whatever ventures I *want* to support and discriminate against those I find inconvenient, embarrassing, or otherwise problematic. There are no practical barriers for me doing so. I'm pretty sure that if a student complains to the Yale administration that I have not supported the student's eyebrow-raising venture, the administration's response would be a resounding shrug. Maybe what is in my self-interest is good enough, period.

That line of thought is sometimes called "ethical egoism." It's the theory that what makes something ethical is merely what is in our own self-interest, and generally things would work out fine if we all just pursued our best interests.[27] If you're a fan of author Ayn Rand, you'll be familiar with ethical egoism.

On the other hand, I've wondered whether I have a duty to support my students' passions. Kierkegaard wrote, "The thing is to find a truth *for me*, to find *the idea for which I can live and die*."[28] Sarah and Matt had found their truths. Sarah was committed to the sexual empowerment of her customers. Matt firmly believed pornography could and should be more ethical. They were clearly passionate about their ideas, and in retrospect, I am uncomfortable that I did not offer them the full support I gave other students.

I believe I have a professional duty to treat students equally. I don't know whether that means I need to support whatever venture students choose, but to do so seems, in my eyes, praiseworthy. It is the kind of educator I want to be.

Finally, Matt's porn venture reminded me that my students and I do not exist in a vacuum. The reason I told my senior colleagues about Matt's venture was because I had some inkling that I had duties to Yale, not just to my students. I was concerned about the fallout Matt's ventures might create for Yale. If his classmates revolted, it would cause a distraction and they would learn less. If his venture became newsworthy, it could be a hassle for the school. It might stoke the ire of illustrious alumni and cause a headache for my decanal colleagues. In light of possible negative outcomes, I wondered whether I had a duty to forewarn my university about Matt's venture. The answer, I think, is yes.

Obligations to the University

Just as I have duties by virtue of my relationship to students, so too do I have duties by virtue of my relationship with my employer, the university. Yale, the "principal," pays me, its "agent," to fulfill the university's mission, or at least the small corner of the mission for which I am responsible. Through my acceptance of my paycheck, I enter into this principal-agent relationship and acquire an obligation to look after Yale's interests—though, as my tales from entrepreneurship education reveal, my duties to my employer can sometimes be brought into conflict with my duties to the students in my care.[29]

I have many duties arising from my principal-agent relationship with Yale, including a duty of loyalty, duty of obedience, and duty to inform. My duty of loyalty to Yale means, generally, that I ought not work against my employer's interests through activities such as engaging in competition with Yale, sabotaging its activities, creating conflicts of interests, or violating the university's confidentiality. Across a variety of countries and cultures, employment law requires that employees "behave during the period of employment so as to enhance, rather than harm or hinder, the business interests of the employer."[30] My duty of obedience is related, and means roughly that I ought to do what I am told.[31] If my dean says we will not be supporting cannabis-related ventures, then I have an obligation to follow that dictum.

The duty to inform is a common component of principal-agent, fiduciary relationships. For example, doctors (agents) have a duty to inform patients (principals) of a bad diagnosis, even if the diagnosis would frighten the patient or there is no treatment. And companies (agents) have a duty to tell shareholders (the principals) about information material to the stock price. My duty to inform as a Yale employee means that I must inform the university of information relevant to the institution's interests. If a student venture could have adverse consequences for the school, for instance, I have a duty to inform the school through its appointed leaders.

The duty to inform is paramount because other duties, such as the duty of obedience, are predicated on the university being informed. How could a university prohibit me from supporting cannabis ventures if I never told the university I was supporting cannabis ventures?

As you saw from my experience with Matt's porn venture, my support of students—whether motivated by ethical duties or merely a desire to be supportive—can come into conflict with my duties to my university. Though I think we should give founders great leeway to choose and support them along their path, I do not think that leeway is boundless. If I use the resources of the university to support a student founder selling meth using the blockchain, I have wronged my employer by implicating them in an illegal activity. I am not vindicated by pleading that I merely worked on the project the student had chosen. At the same time, I would be wrong to turn away students working on controversial ventures merely because they make *me* uncomfortable. Is not the university a bastion of free expression and exploration of new ideas?

Since my experiences with Matt and Sarah as well as a few drug-related ventures, I have erred on the side of informing my university when I fear that by supporting a student, I might run afoul of my duties to Yale. That is most often true when a venture is potentially illegal or embarrassing, but also sometimes when I detect potentially unethical dimensions of a venture.

Unethical Ventures

Sometimes a student venture is not doing anything illegal or embarrassing, but my consequentialist side has the feeling that something is vaguely unethical about its business. Consider JUUL, which began life as an entrepreneurship project in a class at Stanford University. The company is a leading maker of electronic cigarette, or "vaping," products in the United States. It created youth-focused vape flavors, developed marketing attractive to youths, and is widely blamed for the epidemic of youth vaping.[32] Indeed, youths frequently say that they "JUUL" rather than "vape."

There is, I think, a sound argument to be made that JUUL is an unethical venture, particularly if you're a consequentialist: JUUL produces some pretty bad consequences in the world. Mill would not be impressed. And I doubt Stanford is too proud of these founders. There is slim chance that Stanford will ever feature the JUUL founders on the cover of its alumni magazine.

How should educators handle ventures that are potentially unethical? I haven't encountered a student founder with business models they *believed* to be unethical. No student ever told me, "This is unethical, but it's a great business." Perhaps the social norms of our institutions discourage such ventures.

Most potentially unethical ventures I see at universities are those taking advantages of their users, harming their users, or creating what economists call negative externalities, such as pollution or carbon emissions. For example, we might question the ethics of ventures using certain blockchain technologies that are grossly inefficient users of energy. The carbon emissions of the Ethereum blockchain in 2021 was roughly the equivalent of two or three coal-fired power plants.[33] The nicotine-containing vaping products marketed by JUUL are consumed voraciously by customers, but nicotine and the other chemicals in electronic cigarettes are bad for those customers. Ventures selling alcohol are similar. (I've supported a few Yale entrepreneurs who started successful companies selling alcoholic beverages.)

There are lots of other examples. Many video games take advantage of "whales," people with addictive personalities who compulsively make in-app purchases (it costs more than $100,000 to equip one's avatar fully in Activision Blizzard's *Diablo Immortal* video game).[34] Mobile social media apps can have similar adverse effects.[35] We lament the screen addiction of our children, which exposes them to adult content, bullying, FOMO, and unrealistic concepts of body image, lifestyle, and happiness. Ponzi schemes, always a hit with customers, are now much easier to create with blockchain technologies.[36] Other legal but likely unethical business models include those profiting from misinformation or hate speech.[37]

Despite all of these instances, I don't so often see student start-ups with *business models* that are inherently unethical as I see unethical *behavior* by founders in a start-up that is otherwise fine. Elizabeth Holmes, who founded Theranos as a sophomore at Stanford, is the poster child for unethical behavior by a founder. She deceived patients, partners, and investors alike, marketing bogus blood tests for diseases over a multiyear period.[38] It was an extensive and brazen fraud.

Few founders are guilty of *that* level of moral turpitude. Fraud is rare, thankfully. Lesser transgressions are more common, especially playing fast and loose with the truth. This is the ethical transgression for which I most frequently find myself chastising student founders.

I recall first witnessing a founder's loose relationship with truth as a graduate student and budding entrepreneur at MIT, as I listened to one of the Akamai founders speak about his experience. Akamai, a company founded at MIT just a few years before I arrived, is a still-thriving content delivery network that was almost instantly successful. The founder told our roomful of students about his interactions with venture capitalists, boasting that they had been told the company had ten data centers when five was the truth, twenty when there were ten, and so on. It stuck with me.

In "Entrepreneurs and the Truth"—a 2021 article I wrote with my colleagues Tom Byers, Laura Dunham, and Jon Fjeld, also entrepreneurship educators—we described *why* founders bend the truth:

> The norms of entrepreneurship encourage founders to be hustlers and evangelists for their companies. Indeed, legendary founders are celebrated for their ability to inspire others, even if that means stretching the truth. Consider Steve Jobs, the quintessential start-up pitchman. Early Apple employees describe him as able to "convince anyone of practically anything." In the words of engineer Andy Hertzfeld, Jobs had a "reality distortion field, a confounding mélange of a charismatic rhetorical style, an indomitable will, and an eagerness to bend any fact to fit the purpose at hand."[39]

Between harmless puffery and straight-up lies is a menagerie of more minor mendacity we identified, including "obfuscation, lies of omission, exaggeration, embellishment, evasion, bluffs, and half-truths."[40] Entrepreneurship faculty have a front-row seat to these transgressions. Countless times, I have seen a founder obfuscate by judiciously choosing axes on a graph. I regularly hear founders make statements such as "user growth was 20 percent per month from January to June," though the founder knows full well that July was a down month and thus is lying by omission. Founders often exaggerate and embellish the involvement of famous mentors and members of their scientific advisory boards. They deceive when they handpick unrepresentative user quotes. Many founders, having consumed their own Kool-Aid, do these things reflexively, without thought. As German philosopher Friedrich Wilhelm Nietzsche reputedly said, "The visionary lies to himself, the liar only to others."

Where's the line between bullishness and falsehood? I don't know. It's not a bright one. I do know that educators are better able to see that line than young and inexperienced student founders. Faculty have a duty to point out student's falsehoods, however small, and in a larger sense, help student entrepreneurs understand the moral dimensions of their start-up activities. This is a rather ancient component of our responsibilities to students. From the informal school of Socrates to the early US university, ethics was a compulsory component of education.[41] Now in light of the high-profile transgressions of start-ups, some faculty are integrating ethics education explicitly into entrepreneurship education.[42]

It's a difficult job. Most entrepreneurship faculty have on-the-job rather than formal academic training in ethics. Also, faculty have a difficult time addressing ethical questions with student founders because those questions are murky, unclear, open to debate, and rife with uncertainty. JUUL became a terrible social ill, and most people know it as such. But it did not start out like that. If you watch the YouTube video of founders' final project presentation in their Stanford class, you'll likely see them as well-intentioned, smart, and committed to the noble cause of helping smokers consume nicotine without the harm of combusting tobacco.[43] It would be challenging for most educators to have predicted from that presentation what the venture would become.

However difficult the task, helping student founders comport themselves in an ethical manner is worthy and likely required by our fiduciary-like duties to students. Entrepreneurs are not unethical by nature. Indeed, what scant data exist suggest that entrepreneurs are *more* ethical than run-of-the-mill managers.[44] But the immense pressures of entrepreneurship can cause founders to cut ethical corners. Helping entrepreneurs understand the ethical dimension of entrepreneurship can facilitate student founders to do what is *right* when it is difficult to do so.

It can be tempting, especially for business school students, to rationalize ethically dubious behavior as just part of doing business, and believe we exist in a freewheeling, no-holds-barred capitalist arena in which contestants are each responsible for their own welfare and knowing the rules of the game.[45] In the United States, we accept almost as an article of faith that the competitive forces in that arena will produce the greatest good and advance the interests of society, guided by the "invisible hand" described by economist Adam Smith. As it turns out, though, Smith himself didn't share that faith. He considered ethical behavior indispensable, writing in *The Theory of Moral Sentiments*,

> What would become of the duties of justice, of truth, of chastity, of fidelity, which it is so difficult to observe, and which there may be so many strong motives to violate? But upon the tolerable observance of these duties depends the very existence of human society, which would crumble into nothing if mankind were not generally impressed with a reverence for those important rules of conduct.[46]

Recommendations:

- Don't turn away students with bad ventures. Through education, you can help those students understand why their ventures are bad and how to fix them. Further, you can help ensure students do not commit themselves to bad ventures but instead opt for other careers after graduation. They have a lifetime to be entrepreneurs.

- Some students want to build lifestyle ventures—small businesses that don't have the potential for high growth. Such ventures are bad in many ways, but might be the passion of a student's life. If the student clearly understands the downsides of such ventures, educators should support these students as they would other entrepreneurs.

- The foregoing recommendations about lifestyle and bad ventures apply to the ordinary pedagogical resources of the university. To avoid moral hazard or the appearance of endorsement, educators should avoid giving substantial prizes and other extraordinary resources to bad ventures.

- Some students will have ventures that are embarrassing but not illegal, such as my student making sex toys. Educators should support these students, even if it is awkward.

- Some student ventures can have negative consequences for the university, bringing educators' duties to students into conflict with their duties to their universities. At a minimum, educators must inform their universities of such ventures, and if requested, deny these founders support.

- Educators should not be sheepish when it comes to pointing out the ethical transgressions of student founders. In particular, educators should help students understand when they might be breaking the law, and thus potentially imperiling themselves and the university.

6
Start-ups in the Classroom

A few years ago, I taught a software entrepreneurship class in which teams of students were asked to build scalable, software-enabled ventures. The students were graded on their venture proposals, progress during the semester, and final pitches, which were presented to a small panel of investors. It was pretty standard stuff.

Charlotte was one of the best students in my class. She made a ton of progress on her venture during the semester: she hired interns, attracted cofounders, launched a functioning e-commerce website, built a social media audience, and sold scads of cute Japanese curios drop-shipped from China to US consumers.

On our course's final day, students rose one after another to give their pitches and receive feedback from my guest "judges," who appraised each venture using a rubric I provided. When it was Charlotte's turn to pitch, however, who ascended the stage? It was *not* Charlotte.

At first I was confused. Who *was* this person onstage? Was the presenter one of "my" students who had ditched class the entire term? No, I was told, the presenter was a student at Yale, but was not enrolled in my class. They were Charlotte's new cofounder and "chief marketing officer." Charlotte thought it best that they give the pitch for her company.

Some part of me was incredulous, but I was more befuddled than anything else, so I let the student proceed with their presentation. The judges, indifferent, gave the team high scores.

How should I grade such a thing? Can you imagine being in a chemistry, English, or finance class and allowing a student to outsource their final presentation? Ill-humored faculty might haul the offending student before a disciplinary committee merely for trying. And yet here in my entrepreneurship class, I knew something was *different* than in those chemistry, English, and finance classes.

Charlotte did not construct the curios she sold by her own hand. She hadn't shipped them to customers herself. She hadn't coded every line of her website from scratch. Charlotte had not authored every one of her social media posts. And all of that was fine with me. In fact, it was *more* than fine. The job of a start-up CEO is not such minutiae but rather the "big picture" items: raising money, recruiting talent, and setting a vision for the company.[1] Charlotte was a great start-up CEO—and so why would I insist that Charlotte rise before our class to give her final pitch *herself*?

Maybe you'd say I wanted to evaluate Charlotte's presentation skills, but that is not something I had really *taught* her. By what logic would I let her outsource other things, such as her goods or website, and *not* the presentation? Would it have been OK if Charlotte gave the presentation using slides someone else had made for her? For all I knew, other students had their slides outsourced. Why care about the slides anyway? A student's final pitch is not their venture but instead a *picture* of their venture—just as a picture of my grandmother is *not* my grandmother. The pitch is a likeness of the venture, a simulacra, the thinnest veneer of something larger and more substantial.

Of course, everyone can imagine a world in which I instructed students in my entrepreneurship class that they may not enlist the aid of others and they must do all of their own work, including making their own pitches and producing their own slides. Grading would seem to be simpler in such a world, but it would come at a price. If I did so, students with cofounders outside my class would not be able to take the class. I would, perversely, be discriminating against the most mature ventures on campus. A big part of entrepreneurship is leadership: building a team that helps the start-up succeed. A founder who *only* does things themselves is a founder who doesn't get much done. Why would I exclude a founder who is a good leader, attracting others into their venture? That doesn't seem quite right.

My grading conundrum with Charlotte illustrates a more general principle: the *practice* of entrepreneurship and classical norms of the classroom are often an awkward marriage that raises ethical issues. That awkwardness is apparent not only in questions about how to grade entrepreneurship classes but also in many other dilemmas. Should faculty keep student venture information confidential? How should students decide who is a "founder" of a venture birthed in class? Who owns the IP created in class? With each of these questions, it difficult to know what is right, just, and fair. These questions force educators to choose between priorities that are frequently in opposition: the narrow good of our personal interest, the "greatest good" of Mill, and our profession duties to our universities and students, on which Kant might focus.

Grading

My conundrum with Charlotte prompted me to ask myself what I was trying to achieve with my grading. Was it wrong to allow her to outsource her presentation? I wondered whether I should give her a bad grade simply because she had done so, even though she was an excellent entrepreneur and had clearly mastered the course subject matter. What is the "right way" to grade, and what does the grade mean in an entrepreneurship class? Why am I even *giving* a grade?

My interest in these questions led me into the scholarly literature on the ethics and history of grading. I found that grades as we currently know them began at Yale. In the 1800s, Yale started to award students one of four grades: *optimi*, second *optimi*, *inferiores (boni)*, or *pejores*. The A–F system was first used at Harvard University in 1883 and persists today in most US universities.[2] The advent of grading accompanied a great transformation of universities from theology-focused finishing schools for the elite to egalitarian institutions for the masses, offering numerous courses of study—including some that were explicitly vocational.[3]

Today grades serve many purposes. They are an evaluation of a student's mastery of course material. They are also used for admissions, graduation eligibility, merit awards, employment decisions, instructor feedback, and student motivation.[4] That's a lot—in fact, *too much*—to ask of a single letter.

Fair Grades

After much digging, I encountered the works of professors Gary Chartier, Daryl Close, and Gregory Weis, who collectively describe a view of grading that is, I feel, consistent with my ethical duties to students. I summarize their perspectives into four principles, with some small modifications and comments on how this method of grading applies particularly to entrepreneurship.

- "Grading should be based on a student's competence in the academic content of the course."[5]

Nothing else ought to be included. Chartier states that the grade ought to be a point estimate of a student's "subject matter competence" (SMC) and nothing else. He calls this the "principle of academic exclusion."[6] In Chartier's view, a student looking at their grade ought to know the answer to the question, "What is the degree to which I am competent in this subject matter?" Further, persons with whom they choose to share their grade should know the answer to that question as well.

What does it mean that only SMC ought to be included in the grade? It means that many of the factors I included in *my* grading ought not to have been part of my calculus. For example, I would often factor into my grading a student's effort, progress, attendance at office hours, and participation in class. To the extent that I did so, I polluted the grade and thereby in some sense was *lying* to students about their SMC.

In his award-winning "Fair Grades" paper, Close uses the example of a food inspector to show why this is perverse. In many countries, food inspectors assign different grades to foods, ranging from the best-quality foods to those unfit for human consumption. How would we feel about a food inspector giving better grades to food producers who didn't produce quality foods, but tried hard or asked the inspector probing, insightful questions? These things are, of course, irrelevant.

While I find Close's food inspector analogy persuasive, I feel "parachute inspector" is a better analogy for entrepreneurship educators. Before jumping, astute parachutists inspect the state of their equipment, including both their main and backup chutes. For new parachutists, an experienced inspector will do this. As that inspector, I would not tell parachuting novices that their packs look OK merely because they expended much effort in packing the chutes, helped create a good "learning environment" in the parachute-packing class, or attended my parachute-packing office hours. Similarly, I strive to base the grade in my entrepreneurship classes *solely* on students' SMC. I want each student's grade to be an accurate measure of a student's mastery of the subject matter and therefore their preparation for what lies ahead, which for entrepreneurs and parachuters alike, is a perilous endeavor.

- Grading should be impartial and consistent.[7]

This seems like a "no-brainer," but I find entrepreneurship classes and entrepreneurs themselves often create situations in which faculty are tempted to violate this principle. For instance, in my experience, the *best* entrepreneurs are frequently some of the *worst* students; their dedication to their ventures leads them to miss class and assignments. Their excellence as entrepreneurs, however, tempts faculty to treat these students with leniency.

One year, Prisha, a student in one of my entrepreneurship classes, missed multiple quizzes over the course of the term due to engagements for her start-up. I *knew* she was a great entrepreneur. I had even helped her prepare for the investor meetings for which she had ditched my class. I am confident she would have aced the quizzes she missed. So when it was time to assign grades, I was sheepish about assigning her a poor mark because I felt the mark did not reflect her SMC. This created a conundrum. Based on my knowledge, could I give her a better mark? I decided I could not. That would be biased and inconsistent; other students were not afforded the same opportunity as Prisha.

Imagine Prisha's case taken to the extreme. Say Jeff Bezos, the founder of Amazon, enrolls in my entrepreneurship class and completes no work—he just ditches everything. Should I give Bezos an A? I believe an A likely best reflects his SMC, but that's based on my knowledge from *outside class*.

According to the principles of impartiality and consistency, I should base a grade solely on the instruments I administer in class to probe students' SMC. These principles will mostly proscribe makeup work, extra credit, and similar largess—including grade adjustment based on intimate knowledge—dispensed to teachers' favorites.

• Students should give their informed consent to a grading scheme.

I discussed informed consent in chapter 2; it is shorthand for consent that is made voluntarily, competently, and sometimes currently.[8] I don't mean to "trigger" educators by the use of consent here with respect to grading. In practice, this simply means that I must first ensure students understand in advance the scheme by which I will grade them and then have the freedom to opt out of my scheme by dropping the class, or in the case of a required class, have a plausible mechanism of redress for complaints. Adherence to this principle has two nice side effects: it forestalls later drama, and causes me to think through the nature of my assignments and how those assignments are graded. Close goes so far as to say that for a grade to be fair, each component of the grade must be made explicit and numerical, such as "assignment #5 is worth 4.3 percent of your grade." If a class is required and cannot be dropped by students, I think Close's argument for explicit numerical grades is strong.

- "Grades should be assigned on the basis of an expert evaluation of student work."[9]

If I let my eldest child grade my students' assignments, that would be intuitively unfair because my child, though precocious, is not an expert in entrepreneurship. Further, grading students myself by randomly throwing darts against a board or drawing grades from a hat would also be unfair because I would not have employed my own expertise. Letting students grade each other is similarly flawed. My expertise relative to students is part of what distinguishes me as a faculty person and creates my fiduciary-like obligations to the students. One of those obligations is that I *use* my expertise in evaluating students.

Returning to my parachute inspector example, were I to tell students that they know how to pack their parachutes safely when in fact they do not, I would imbue them with a dangerous false notion. I would be lying to them. As Arlen Gullickson observes, "When student evaluations are poor, not sound, they victimize and harm students academically, economically, and socially."[10] In general, then, to the degree that I use my expertise to provide students with grades that are an accurate estimate of their SMCs, I better fulfill my obligations to students.

Participation and Other Inaccurate Instruments

Grading based on SMC is difficult because each student's SMC is hidden in their skull. It is a latent variable; I can no more *see* students' SMC than I can *see* how much they love their parents. Since I cannot directly observe students' SMC, I must design "instruments" by which SMC can be probed and estimated. Not all such instruments are the equal. Some, like quizzes and exams, are relatively accurate, whereas others, such as group projects and class participation, are relatively inaccurate, and therefore poor choices for educators committed to giving students grades that reflects their individual SMC.

I once had occasion to review a faculty person at another university as part of his promotion process. For the review, I read the syllabus of this faculty person's entrepreneurship class and learned that students' grade in his class were computed as follows: 65 percent of the grade was based on the "class project," and 35 percent was based on "participation and attendance." The class project required a five-page paper and ten-slide pitch for each *team* of students working together on a venture.

I submit to you that it is entirely possible for a student to have a *terrible* SMC yet get a good grade in that class. Likewise, a student could have *great* competency and still get a poor grade. That's because both measures are terrible instruments for measuring SMC, just in different ways.

For now, let me focus on participation. That participation and its precondition, attendance, are inaccurate instruments for measuring SMC should be obvious: a student may master the course material and yet choose to sit silently in class or not attend class at all. So why do entrepreneurship faculty often include a participation component in their grading scheme? Chartier discusses two reasons. The first is what he calls "academic consequentialism," of which he describes two types:

> Someone committed to general academic consequentialism will make grading decisions with the purpose of bringing about the greatest possible amount of good in the universe, whereas, someone committed to restricted academic consequentialism will make grading decisions with the purpose of bringing about the greatest possible amount of some more narrowly specified good.[11]

A consequentialist grader employs two rationales in saying that students must attend class and participate: it will help create a better learning environment for all, and individual students will increase their own learning by doing so. As Weis puts it, "Both we professors and our institutions often speak of the importance of student attendance and participation in our courses. We inform students that they have an obligation to help make our courses 'happen,' to help create an atmosphere in which teaching and learning can take place."[12]

I confess to the error of using both attendance and participation in this manner. I know that these behaviors are poor instruments for measuring student SMC. Indeed, in my experience, attendance is often *negatively* correlated with SMC; the best entrepreneurs in my courses are the students most frequently late or absent because they're off meeting with customers and investors during class time.

Chartier explains a second reason for which faculty factor in attendance:

> Academic retributionism is the concept that a grade may in part rightly reflect a moral judgment regarding a student's character as it manifests itself in academic contexts. Under academic retributivism, a grade may be in part a means of rewarding a student for morally good academic conduct and punishing her for morally bad academic conduct.[13]

Is tardiness, disrupting class, or absenteeism morally praiseworthy? No. Will these serve students well in their lives? Of course not. The academic retributionist uses the punishment of a low grade to discourage condemnable behaviors, *even if* that behavior is not an accurate measure of the student's SMC, and encourage praiseworthy behaviors such as participation.

Close even takes the outré view that *cheating* ought not to be punished through grades; the A student who lets another student copy their answers does not deserve a lower grade but instead should suffer some administrative consequence, such as receiving an "incomplete." To give that student a lower grade is to *lie* about their SMC.

I discovered a third reason that faculty choose to grade participation when a professor from another business school visited Yale to discuss, among other topics, best practices in grading. She told us participation was *half or more* of the grade in the many courses at their school. I pressed her as to why, and she responded with a rationale that I only now understand as the classic consequentialist and to a lesser extent retributionist arguments for grading participation. Toward the end of their visit, almost as an aside, she mentioned that teaching assistants (TAs) at her school were mostly prohibited from grading homework, quizzes, and exams. Aha! This seemed to reveal the *true* reason for the rosy view of participation among their school's faculty: grading participation is *relatively* easy. Who among faculty people, required to grade all of their assignments, would create many assignments? A masochist? A saint?

I understand that her school made this rule for good reasons: to prevent students from grading each other and ensure that grading was done by the faculty person, who is the most qualified individual. This rule, however, had the perverse effect of encouraging faculty to create *fewer* assignments and other instruments by which they could accurately measure a student's SMC.

I suspect that most other faculty people share with me feeling *good* when students participate and feeling *bad* when they don't, thus making a certain *selfishness* the fourth reason we grade based on participation. I have an inkling that these feelings are amplified in entrepreneurship classes, which more than classes in other areas, incorporate guests. I often invite famous entrepreneurs and investors into my classroom to help the students understand how what we're learning in *theory* is manifest *in practice*. I am grateful for the precious time these illustrious guests donate to our school and their contribution to the education of our students—and am mortified when, on occasion, my students stare mutely at our guests, unable to articulate interesting questions.

I can imagine that other faculty people feel what I do when this sort of thing happens: a strong temptation to use grades to motivate participation. It is a temptation to avoid.

Participation is not only an inaccurate measure of a student's SMC but also a tough thing to measure "correctly." How should I grade a question that betrays a lack of understanding from a student? Should I give higher grades for questions or statements that show mastery? If I do so, what space is left for students to ask "dumb" questions?

I have in the past asked my TAs to record and reward students for participation that "moves the class discussion forward." For example, I instructed the TAs to award high marks to student comments that demonstrated mastery of the material, but also to comments and questions that unearthed widespread misunderstandings or prompted healthy dialogue. My nuanced instructions made it *more* difficult for TAs to grade participation. How are my young TAs to know whether a question failed to stimulate dialogue or if I just needed to move on to the next topic?

I now understand the difficulty of relying on TA expertise rather than my own to grade participation. Grading participation on my own, though, is tricky too. First, it is just logistically difficult. Ought I write down marginal additions to a student's participation score in the moment that they participate? My colleague did that. After a student spoke, he'd say, "Great, ten points" or "No, that's wrong, one point," and the TA would record the student's marks. The effect was simultaneously hilarious and chilling. Most faculty can't interrupt class to record participation in the moment. And yet if I do not, I am at risk of forgetting students' contributions. Further, my perception of students' participation is surely biased; I am likely to reward students whose views agree with mine or those students who fill uncomfortable silences, relieving my unease.

I've looked back at my grading of participation in the past and regret it. I found that those with the highest participation grades rarely had the highest grades on other assignments that are more accurate measures of SMC. I want my classroom to be a learning environment, not a theater for the loquacious. I have since diminished the importance of participation and tweaked how I grade it, without removing it entirely from my grading schemes. Where possible, I try to use social rewards to encourage participation. For example, in some classes I have TAs take notes about students' contributions so that I can send individualized follow-up emails thanking students for their contributions. I also try to recognize students for outstanding contributions in front of their peers and make sure not to shame those who demonstrate a lack of mastery through their participation. This revised approach is a work in progress.

Peer Grading

I can dispense with peer grading quite easily. The simple fact is that students lack the expertise to assess each other's SMC accurately. Plus, I can attest to just how problematic peer grading really is because I am personally guilty of the most egregious use of it you'll likely ever hear about, from the time years ago when I went "whole hog" into peer grading while teaching an entrepreneurship course in computer science with my colleague. It's a cautionary tale.

In an effort to make our class more realistic, my colleague and I designed a "stock market" for the student ventures. Each start-up in class had a single "CEO" founder who was locked into their venture. Other students could work for whomever they chose and change teams at will; they could also trade "shares," thereby setting the fluctuating price for each start-up's "equity." Students' grades were largely determined by the value of equity they managed to acquire by the end of the semester.

This scheme quickly turned the classroom into *Lord of the Flies*. Students engaged in backroom dealings working for multiple start-ups, the best developers in the class received enormous "pay" packages, and a few students were orphaned, unwelcome in any start-up. As models of the "real world" go, it wasn't bad, but it was an unethical way for me to grade. In retrospect, I'm just happy that no student reported me. Lesson learned.

My argument is not that peer grading ought to be banned entirely. It's that peer grading is less accurate than faculty grading and often less fair. Of course, there is sometimes pedagogical value in having students evaluate each other's work. But to the extent that influences grades, it ought to do so only sparingly. Returning to my parachute inspector metaphor, it is certainly fine and harmless to have first-time jumpers inspect each other's packs. But it would be madness for the instructor to let them jump on that basis.

Grading Projects

Projects are particularly prominent components of classes in entrepreneurship for a few reasons. One is that we—entrepreneurship educators, entrepreneurs, and perhaps the entire world—feel that entrepreneurship must *actually be done* to be understood. It is like riding a bicycle. I could teach you all about physics, how gears work, how to maintain and build a bike, the technique of pedaling and turning, and so on, but having done all of that, it would be wrong to say that you know *how to ride a bike*. Indeed, with that sort of biking "education," you're apt to fall flat on your face.

Like bike riding, entrepreneurship education is about more than merely facts, but something different—what philosopher Gilbert Ryle called *know-how*. In a seminal address he gave in 1945 to the Aristotelian Society, Ryle differentiated *knowing how* from *knowing that*, with the latter being what you get in a typical lecture class:

"maxims, imperatives, regulative propositions, prescriptions, canons, recipes, rules, theories."[14] This is also called "propositional knowledge." Knowing how, in contrast, is some kind of ineffable, practical capacity to excel that must be acquired by practice.[15]

Most people have the intuitive sense that entrepreneurship—like bike riding, playing the violin, or woodworking—involves a lot of know-how, which explains why entrepreneurship classes have a lot of venture projects. We think you need to *do* entrepreneurship to gain this know-how.

How do we ascertain a student's SMC from an in-class entrepreneurship project such as a venture? It's difficult, for two reasons.

First, entrepreneurship educators typically have *groups* undertake venture projects in class because they know that single-founder start-ups are rare and rarely successful. Doing so has the effect of obscuring individual students' SMC: students with a low SMC can free ride on their peers; students with a high SMC are dragged down by those free riders; and many ventures have outside contributors who are not enrolled in class, including employees, interns, consultants, and cofounders. It is challenging to discern accurately a single student's SMC by observing a team's collective output.

Second, numerous exogenous factors unrelated to students' SMC influence a venture's success. Typically, a student team will receive higher marks if its in-class venture is successful—that is, its founders do the kinds of things successful start-ups do: attract customers, raise money, prove hypotheses about their business, and so on. These, however, are only loosely correlated with *mastery*. For example, would a student in an entrepreneurship class receive a high grade for successfully closing a round of funding? Does that demonstrate mastery of the material? Perhaps. Mastery certainly doesn't *hurt* in fundraising, but the ease of raising money differs dramatically by market. In the early 2020s, a lobotomized sophomore with fifty lines of code and only the thinnest entrepreneurship know-how could raise a preseed round for a "crypto" venture.

Further, a student's prior access to capital can help them raise money. A student with rich parents will likely have access to more capital through their social network, irrespective of their merit in class and mastery of the material. I recall one year speaking with Marsha, a student in my entrepreneurship class. As I had done for her classmates, I taught her how she could build a website cheaply herself. But she wasn't interested; she told me she had $300,000 to spend on exploring her idea and building her website.

Marsha, it turned out, came from a superwealthy family. And she made a ton of progress with that $300,000 during our semester. I don't think Marsha knew any more about entrepreneurship than the other student founders, but she surely left her classmates in the dust with her progress. And she got a great grade. What percentage of her progress was due to her deep pockets? It wasn't zero.

Venture progress takes many forms, including sales closed, financing raised, team members hired, and pitch contests won. These are each influenced by numerous factors, of which a student's entrepreneurship SMC is only one. That's why venture progress is an imperfect measure of SMC and basis for grades.

"Fixing" this problem is difficult and impractical. Imagine I want to make grading easier so I say that all members of a venture must be enrolled in a class; you can't have cofounders outside class. By doing so, I would prevent some of *best* ventures and entrepreneurs from enrolling. That seems perverse and undesirable. Or imagine that I want to eliminate the fixed effects of markets so I say, "This class is only for start-ups in XYZ market." Would our school then require ten other classes for start-ups in other markets?

Project grading using commercial metrics of success surely rewards "success," but not necessarily *learning*. Picture a student team that begins a project-based class with a dead-end idea—which describes many of them. The team articulates hypotheses about its business, designs experiments, and comes to understand the shortfalls of its initial idea. It pivots to a second idea and maybe even a third before the semester's end. The students on this team can develop *real mastery* of entrepreneurship concepts and yet lack commercial indications of success. Their high SMC will seem to be contradicted by their low grades.

As if the innate problems with projects were not bad enough, entrepreneurship educators often compound them by outsourcing grading to panels of investors—and making how those investors rate a pitch a hefty fraction of students' grades. My entrepreneurship class with the student Charlotte, described at this chapter's beginning, is an example. I had investors grade my student's pitches, based on a rubric I provided, which included ratings on a zero-to-ten scale on dimensions such as "customer/problem is clear," "solution solves customer's problem," and "team understands competition."

That might be a decent way to pick a winner in a pitch competition, but it was a terrible way for me to estimate students' SMC and settle on grades. Imagine teaching music and bringing in professional musicians to grade a performance. One judge is an expert in Chinese opera, another is an expert in the music of Canadian First Peoples, and still another an expert in a rock music. You can see how it would be problematic to employ these judges' evaluations to grade the second violinist playing in a string quartet.

Like musicians, investors have different preferences, knowledges, and pet peeves. Their grading is often all over the place. They also have all manner of biases. Take *gender*, for example; we know that investors (regardless of their own gender identity) generally prefer male founders, and prefer that women founders fit into gender stereotypes (e.g., women, stereotyped as "caregivers," as founders for social ventures).[16] Research even shows that investors score pitches higher when male founders are handsome (but aren't swayed by women's appearance).[17]

Of course, faculty have their own biases. But students have mechanisms for redress of bias from faculty. For instance, faculty can be denied promotion, pay, and other privileges by administrators empowered to police the discriminatory treatment of students. No such redress exists for students facing investors.

In retrospect, maybe Charlotte's decision to outsource her pitch to my panel of investors was astute. After all, I had outsourced my grading.

To recap, our problem as educators is that learning entrepreneurship requires know-how and acquiring know-how requires "doing," like through projects. Projects, though, are a poor way to establish an *individual* student's SMC and therefore we are likely to give an unfair grade—a grade that is a poor estimator of a student's SMC.

The situation can be fixed. To do so, first, you should think of class projects as vehicles through which students *learn*, but *not* as instruments through which you can measure students' SMC with much accuracy. Chartier makes this distinction:

> There is no hard-and-fast distinction between practice-oriented, skill-building homework exercises and others, which serve primarily to facilitate the accurate assessment of SMC, such as in-class examinations. However, it is clear that some homework exercises are designed primarily to help students acquire proficiencies of various sorts instead of measuring SMC.

And further, Chartier notes,

> In accordance with the PAE, an instructor should where possible, avoid basing grades on students' performance on repetitive, skill-building exercises. Instructors should assign such exercises where appropriate, but they may violate the PAE when used to estimate students' SMC and in determining their grades.[18]

Chartier's argument is simple: some things students do in class are good for promoting learning, and some things are good for measuring students' SMC—but those things are *not necessarily* the same. This is a tough pill to swallow for entrepreneurship educators. It is a convenient fiction to believe that we can compute a student's SMC accurately if we listen to a five-minute pitch and read a short executive summary. Moreover, students are complicit in helping us educators live in that fiction; they aren't exactly clamoring for more essays and exams. What student doesn't love practice-focused entrepreneurship classes? No one wants to take some "lame" entrepreneurship class that has exams and stuff.

How can we give grades that are better reflections of students' SMC and thus do better at fulfilling our duties as educators? Unfortunately, there is no silver bullet. It requires those essays and exams, quizzes, arduous grading, and other unpleasant work by both faculty and students. In my own classes, I ensure that group projects are—to the extent I can make them so—large parts of the students' learning experience but small parts of their grade. I also integrate quizzes, exams, and similar instruments that provide *relatively* accurate measurements of students' SMC. These are *not* popular. And it requires a ton of work to create, administer, and grade such things. In the end, however, a grade that more accurately reflects each student's SMC is worth the effort.

Faculty Confidentiality

I regularly receive inquiries from investors about student founders in my classes. These investors are typically also donors, friends, or others with whom I have substantial social ties. They want to know what I think about this or that particular student. Is the student's venture good? They want to know whether they should be interested or if the particular student is best avoided.

I know a *ton* about my students and their ventures, and so I usually have answers to these questions. But here's the problem: I acquired most of what I know about my students and their ventures in environments that students likely presumed were confidential—especially our private meetings to discuss their ventures' progress.

When I meet with students in my entrepreneurship classes, I compel them to be candid with me, explaining that doing so is necessary for my grading. Therefore I see the "sausage being made": their failed prototypes, lost customers, tepid adoption, cofounder disputes, and vacillating commitment to the venture. Working through these struggles is a major part of the students' learning process.

There are a few reasons I am compelled to keep *most* of this information confidential—and other entrepreneurship educators should do the same. One is that if you teach in the United States, it is likely *illegal* to share all sorts of information about students without their prior written consent. US institutions that receive federal funding—and almost every university in the country does—are bound by the Family Educational Rights and Privacy Act (FERPA) and its amendments.[19] FERPA requires universities and their educators to obtain prior written consent before sharing most information about a student, including name, class list, grades, disciplinary records, and other personally identifiable information. While there are exceptions for law enforcement, immigration officials, parents of students under eighteen, and national security officials, there are no exceptions for angel investors, venture capitalists, or rich alumni.

FERPA is unambiguous for US educators. You need written consent to tell anyone that a student is in your class, that a student in your class is a top performer, or that a student in your class has poor moral caliber.[20] Things are less onerous when it comes to *extracurricular* activities—student participation that is not similarly protected. So, for example, educators running an extracurricular summer accelerator would *not* be prohibited by FERPA from sharing information about the student founders in the program.

Another reason I keep student information confidential, whether I acquired it through curricular or extracurricular activities, has to do with the nature of that information and how students themselves may choose to share it. For instance, students tell me much more than they tell investors—at least initially. I compel students to show me the ugliness of the sausage-making process precisely because that ugliness is part of their education in entrepreneurship.

I should note that I often accompany these same students when they pitch to investors, where they tell a *different* story. The investors get the polished version, free of blemishes and caveats. This isn't deception; rather, the students are merely putting their best foot forward, choosing for themselves the content and character of what investors hear.[21]

If I share a student's potentially confidential information with an investor, I rob that student of the chance to describe their venture themselves, in the manner of their choosing. By betraying what I know of how the sausage is made, I infringe on the student's autonomy. (For a more thorough discussion of the role of faculty as intermediaries between students and investors or other service providers, see chapter 4.)

My final reason for keeping student information confidential is that I likely have an ethical obligation to do so due to my fiduciary-like relationship with the student. I need to look out for students' best interests, just as doctors, lawyers, and therapists are expected to do for their clients. Imagine if my boss plumbed my therapist for information about me, and my therapist dished, "Kyle pulls the wings off flies in his basement and has daddy issues." It would clearly be a violation of the trust I placed in them. Even a therapist offering my employer the relatively vague advice to "avoid Kyle" would still have betrayed me. Similarly, students put their trust in their educators while receiving an education. In so doing, the student may make all manner of mistakes as well as display all manner of ignorance and immaturity. We should keep those things confidential.

The tough part is that we also need to keep student information confidential *even if it is positive*. I should not pick and choose what I can tell investors using consequentialist logic. I shouldn't be deciding that this or that might be harmful to pass along, and that something else might be helpful.

I do my utmost to avoid sharing student information with investors, whether that information is good or bad. This choice, however, creates some challenges. For instance, I must be careful *how* I avoid sharing information. I learned that lesson early in my teaching career when an investor said something to me like, "I hear Clare is in your class. She came to see me, and I liked her venture. We're thinking about investing." I changed the subject, keen to avoid giving any signal to this investor.

That night, a colleague of mine who was friends with the investor called me and said that the investor was spooked because I didn't sing Clare's praises. From the investor's perspective, my unwillingness to discuss Clare was a coded *negative* signal. Crud. In fact, Clare was a *fine* entrepreneur, and I think her venture would have made a *fine* investment. I violated my commitment to confidentiality and called the investor to fix the mess I created.

Since then, I err on the side of verbosity when avoiding questions about students. I will give investors a lengthy spiel when time allows. I explain that I am grateful for an investor's interest in our students and that our students are a fantastic lot about whom I care deeply. I state that I am committed to keeping student venture information confidential so that students can be candid with me and I can help them to my fullest capacity. Then I ask for the potential investor's forgiveness for not answering their questions and assure them that I wouldn't answer no matter who the question was about, including the best student founders.

It's difficult to stick to my tight-lipped system. Not long before this writing, an active venture investor told me in passing that they were considering investing in a student venture that I knew to be a train wreck. I wanted to warn them off, but I kept silent. I can only hope that their firm is filled with adults who can look after themselves and uncover bad ventures. I also hope they don't hold it against me for not warning them.

My commitment to confidentiality is not winning me any popularity contests. I am certain that investors in my community think I'm uptight and obtuse, and perhaps I am. I know a few educators who take a different approach, offering uniform praise for all of their students. I can understand that approach, but it doesn't work for me because I'm unwilling to perjure myself by endorsing a train wreck of a student venture.

Student confidentiality and concerns about that confidentiality are even tricky to manage *internally* at the university. For example, imagine that I'm working with Sheri, a student in my class who is developing a mobile app for waste truck drivers. In a different class, my student Balazs wants to create a similar app. (I put these hypothetical students "in class" because it helps my argument that follows, but I think the reasoning prevails even if they are students seeking aid outside class.) Should I tell Balazs about Sheri's venture? Imagine further that Sheri and I worked together, and through her customer discovery process, unearthed important insights about the market. Should I share those conclusions with Balazs? If I do *not* share those insights with Balazs, do I then allow him to pursue dead-end strategies despite my knowing full well how those will turn out? Or imagine that Sheri develops sales leads at a local company. Do I tell that to Balazs? In an ideal world, Balazs and Sheri will join forces, and maybe these problems go away. But Balazs and Sheri may have logical reasons for not working together.

My point is that sometimes my fiduciary-like duties to two students are brought into conflict—here, my duty of confidentiality to Sheri and my duty to look after Balazs's best interests. Such conflicts are common in hot markets and on teams with disputes over ownership or strategic direction.

I find that many first-time founders are hyperconcerned with confidentiality, and they are wrong to be so (more on this in the following section). Having said that, it is not *my place* to shatter a student founder's secrecy. My obligation as an educator is confidentiality for the student. I maintain this confidentiality even after students graduate—although typically at that point, I am willing to speak with investors if the founders grant permission.

Classroom Chaos

Entrepreneurship classrooms are a breeding ground for what Esther Barron and Darren Green have called "early-stage chaos." This is because "students who otherwise have no real ties to one another and never intended to launch a new business end up thrust into an early stage venture as co-founders, leading to a litany of unexpected challenges not typically encountered by companies started under more traditional circumstances."[22] Putting aside whether students in the classes are indeed "cofounders" as used above, there is a lot of truth in that quote.

My own introduction to entrepreneurship came when I was a PhD student in chemical engineering at MIT. "The Institute" was then, and remains today, one of the best places on earth to start a technology company. Early in my studies, my roommate and I took an entrepreneurship class at MIT's Sloan School of Management in which we worked on a biotech idea of his that would morph, years later, into our company, Agrivida.

One of the amazing things about MIT's entrepreneurship environment is how well mixed it is. That Sloan class had students studying engineering, science, medicine, policy, business . . . you name it. One of the students was studying law at Harvard and joined our team for the semester. He was a more polished presenter than we were, but otherwise his contributions were—and here I am being generous—*crap*. The class ended without us having made substantial progress, but it was fun nonetheless.

My roommate and I took other entrepreneurship-related classes and participated in many extracurricular programs as we fleshed out our biotech idea. It was maybe a year after that initial class at Sloan before we began to get traction and decided to incorporate. Sometime around then, we received a legalese-laden letter from our erstwhile classmate, the law student, demanding an equity stake in whatever venture we were founding. The nerve! My cofounder and I had *never* discussed equity or founder status with this student, and had seen neither hide nor hair of him since our class. He contended, however, that working together in class—remember, a class in which *his* contributions were crap—created an implied contract and he was entitled to his pound of flesh.

I was incredulous, but only briefly, for the matter was swiftly sorted. My cofounder and I complained to the Harvard Law School dean, who was kind enough to tell our erstwhile classmate that his claim was without merit.

Entrepreneurship educators have, as Barron and Green observed and I mentioned earlier, "a front row seat to founder intellectual property disputes, equity split disagreements among former students and all manner of other early-stage chaos."[23] I often find myself, now in the shoes of an entrepreneurship educator, adjudicating disputes between students in entrepreneurship classes. In the sections that follow, I discuss the "chaos" relating to ownership of the ideas and work products produced in entrepreneurship classes.

Confidentiality and the Ownership of Ideas

Would-be and first-time founders are frequently paranoid that others will steal their start-up ideas. To these uninitiated entrepreneurs, that seems like a reasonable concern: there's no legal protection for mere *ideas* in the United States and most other countries. Ideas are what you might call *informal* IP, which is different than *formal* IP—the sort that is protected by laws such as copyrights, trademarks, trade secrets, and patents. The only way you can protect an idea is to get others to *agree* to protect it. So, for example, if you worry that I might steal your idea of a "web3" social network for dogs, you can insist that I sign an agreement before you tell me about it in which I promise not to steal your idea or tell other people about it. The same goes for other information you want to keep confidential, such as customer information, sales data, or whatever. The contract or "agreement" a founder uses for this purpose is usually called a confidentiality agreement or NDA.

What kind of confidentiality ought students expect in the classroom? Above, I looked at the confidentiality that students can expect from faculty and other educators; these people ought to maintain students' *classroom* confidentiality quite strictly. That is, students ought to be able to presume the confidentiality of faculty and other educators. Yet students *cannot* presume confidentiality from their peers. (Also, the faculty's obligations to students are looser if students are participating in *cocurricular* entrepreneurship activities, which I discuss in chapter 7.) Considering students' fears of losing their ideas to others, should faculty insist students sign NDAs with *each other* or the university as a condition for participating in entrepreneurship classes? I think the balance of evidence suggests *generally no*.

Three arguments controvert the use of NDAs in class. First, secrecy is overrated; as the adage goes, *ideas are cheap, execution is everything.*[24] A founder with an idea has little about which to be overly proud. They are like a marathoner who has only just tied their laces. For that founder, just at the start, secrecy can even be *harmful*. Rather than keeping their ideas secret or operating in "stealth mode," most founders are better served by being vocal, omnipresent advocates for their ventures. That's how founders find team members, customers, and investors.

Of course, there are exceptions; public disclosure of an invention makes it not patentable in most countries.[25] (The United States provides a one-year grace period after public disclosure, during which you can still get a patent.) But even if a founder's business idea is based on a patentable invention, that founder does not usually need to disclose the inner workings of their invention to garner the interest of others. For example, a student seeking cofounders may reveal that they've discovered how to do cold fusion in their dorm room without disclosing precisely *how* the feat was achieved. The founder so doing would preserve their patent privileges while also living by two of the ancient Greek maxims inscribed at Delphi: "Pursue what is profitable" and "Keep deeply the top secret."[26] Although, as I said, for student founders who have not invented a proverbial "cold fusion," secrecy is more often harmful than helpful.

The second practical argument that controverts the use of NDAs in class is that their protection is illusory because NDAs are notoriously difficult to enforce.[27] If Bill feels as if Ann violated an NDA she signed with him, what practical recourse does he have? Because the NDA is just a contract between two private parties, violating an NDA is a *civil* rather than *criminal* offense in most countries. Bill is on his own to bring a lawsuit against Ann—and what student has the resources and time for *that*? Further, Ann will have diverse defenses: she learned the information elsewhere; she had the same idea; and Bill's NDA was overly general. Bill's tort, in short, has little hope.

Since Bill is a toothless counterparty, imagine instead that the university made students sign NDAs, compelling students in a particular course to keep each other's information confidential. Although the university surely has more resources than Bill, it's difficult to imagine a university making a habit of *suing* its students for violating NDAs, especially because such a university would struggle to establish that it had been harmed in such a way as to justify a tort. I imagine that if a university sued a student for violating a course-mandated NDA, the subsequent newspaper coverage and alumni backlash would ensure that such a lawsuit would never be filed again. Yale's general counsel would laugh me out of their office if I asked them to sue a student (not that they would have let me compel students to sign NDAs in the first place).

My third argument against using NDAs in the classroom is more personal than the first two. It seems to me that NDAs are anathema to academia's spirit of free inquiry and exploration.

Robert M. Hutchins, longtime president and then chancellor of the University of Chicago from the late 1920s to the early 1950s, observed that "free inquiry is indispensable to the good life, that universities exist for the sake of such inquiry, [and] that without it they cease to be universities."[28] Some may say that NDAs enable *freer* inquiry because student founders are more apt to share when their ideas are protected. But were that true, we would likely see their adoption in other IP-heavy domains at universities, such as in writing, art, music, and theater classes.

I have never heard of such a thing. Instead, I think the first-order effect of NDAs is that implied by their plain language: NDAs stifle the transmission of information. And such information is critical in the classroom. For example, many students alter their ideas or "pivot" based on the insights of others offered in class. Surely educators wish to foster such progress rather than sow worry about the ownership of marginal improvements and insights.

For me, NDAs are a bridge too far: an encroachment of the market into the classroom that stifles free inquiry in a manner that I will not abide. So I eschew NDAs in class. In contrast, I tell students just what I wrote above and that they're free to avoid disclosing that which they consider confidential.

I believe my approach is consistent with this advice offered in the *Journal of Management Education*:

> Entrepreneurship instructors should not use written nondisclosure agreements to protect sensitive information. Instead, the professor should provide a verbal standard of nondisclosure as the course norm. Instructors should present this norm from the standpoint of normative ethics, from which one derives desirable and transferable business practices.[29]

I tell student founders that they should respect each other's confidentiality *even without* an NDA. The students should, if only for selfish reasons, develop their bona fides, the traditional Roman virtue describing one's capacity to skillfully put trust in others and be worthy of others' trust in return.[30] After all, entrepreneurship is a "repeated game" in which a student's classmates of today could be their cofounders, competitors, or customers of tomorrow.

Copyrights

In the United States, ideas are not protected by any formal IP right. Documents such as presentations and reports, however, receive *copyright* protection "instantly" at the time of creation. No one is required to *apply* for a copyright; something you write is yours, and you have the right to attempt to prevent others from using your work without your permission.

Here's how this might work in an entrepreneurship class. Let's say Nala tells the class that she thinks it would be a great business to sell environmentally friendly razor blades to climate-conscious consumers through a subscription service and then her classmate Camila turns that idea into a business plan. Camila is the owner of the copyright on that business plan, and Nala isn't the owner of much of anything, even though she had the idea. Nala can't just run off with the business plan Camila wrote.

That said, practically speaking, it would be difficult for Camila to do anything about it if Nala ran off with Camila's business plan. Most copyright infringement is a matter of civil law in the United States, just as is the case with NDAs; Camila has no way of proactively precluding Nala from absconding with her business plan. Camila can only sue for compensation later, after some damage has been done, and that is both difficult and expensive. Of course, Nala has the option of writing a *new*, different business plan *in her own words*.

If Nala and Camila jointly create a presentation, they own that work jointly and equally. Either of them can use that work as though they owned it outright themselves *without* the permission of the other person. So if Camila turns out to be a poor cofounder,

Nala could later start a company alone and use the classwork she created with Camila without worry.

(I have some advice for Nala and Camila regarding their copyrights, which I discuss after introducing the problem of patents.)

Patent Rights

In a survey of US university students published in 2021, 77 percent said they would advise a peer to avoid starting a business while in school for fear that the university might claim ownership of that business.[31] Alas, until recently, founders' fears of covetous colleges were quite credible. It's not that universities make a habit of stealing student's ideas for a new lunch-serving food cart, but numerous universities *have* asserted broad ownership over students' IP through policies that in hindsight, look like little more than "theft of student intellectual property."[32] Fortunately, fewer universities behave this way now.[33]

As I explored in chapter 2, universities ought not seek equity or similar compensation from students who start businesses while in school using merely the ordinary resources of the university—resources to which students are entitled in exchange for their tuition. Similarly, universities ought not expropriate student IP arising through students' use of ordinary university resources.

I am embarrassed to say that Yale was among the patent-acquisitive universities for many years. As the story goes, some of my colleagues in our technology transfer unit convinced the administration that students could not possibly be inventors of patentable innovations in class. Surely, they claimed, the instructor was the inventor—or at least coinventor. That being the case, any patents arising from said invention would be the property of the university because like scientists working in industry, faculty at most universities have agreements with their universities in which faculty proactively agree to assign their patent rights to their institutions. (It is a common misperception that faculty in the United States are *required* by the 1980 Patent and Trademark Law Amendments Act—better known as the Bayh-Dole Act—to assign their IP to their universities. But while IP assignment is commonly required for employment, it is not required by Bayh-Dole.)[34] Students generally have no such agreement—although students at Yale agree to abide by the university's policies.

My colleagues in tech transfer thought that was enough: if Yale's policies said the university would own IP students invented in the classroom, then it would be so. I argued that by that same logic, we could require *anything* of students. How could students be bound by policies they never sign and that could be updated unilaterally? Fortunately, after a few years and a few difficult student-faculty disputes, Yale decided its position was untenable. My colleagues in tech transfer were graceful in their retreat and helped draft a reasonable policy in which students were told explicitly that the university would not attempt to lay claim to patentable inventions or other IP students produce in class. Many other universities did the same around the same time.

This makes sense. A university does not claim to own a poem written in its English classes, so why would it claim to own patents and other IP arising from entrepreneurship classes? In two cases, however, universities *are* justified in their request to take ownership of student-generated IP. First, if students become employees of the university, they will typically be required to sign an IP assignment agreement, just like faculty and staff. That is reasonable; the university pays cash today, with certainty, and in return receives the formal IP derived from the employee's work. Second, universities reasonably claim ownership of or some stake in patentable inventions made by students using the extraordinary resources of the university. These are, as I discussed in chapter 2, the kinds of resources no student could expect to use merely by paying tuition and otherwise maintaining good standing. For example, if a student wishes to use a rare and expensive microscope, the university might rightly insist on owning IP derived from the student's use.

Assuming the university is not involved, how should students apportion their patent rights in the unlikely event that they create something patentable in class? Unlike copyrights on presentations and written work, patent rights are not automatic. If Nala and Camila invent something together in class, they can only establish protection for that invention by submitting a patent application to the US Patent and Trademark Office showing in detail how their invention meets the statutory requirements for being granted a patent. It's an expensive endeavor and takes a while too.

In my experience, students don't often create patentable inventions in class, while almost all students will create material subject to copyright. But imagine that Nala and Camila believe they created a patentable invention in class. They must first determine who is an inventor in the very specific legal sense.[35] If they are each an inventor, they will need to submit their patent application *jointly*. If the patent is granted, they are *each* able to use the rights endowed by the patent *separately*, just as with copyright. If they do not agree that they are joint inventors, they can each file separate patent applications and litigate their cases before the Patent and Trademark Office and potentially in the US court system. Of course, unless a student invents cold fusion in class, that is unlikely to happen.

Informing students of their rights precludes later disputes. I try to achieve roughly informed consent, a concept I talked about previously. Students should understand how the activities in my course will affect their current and future IP rights *before* they get too far into the term. At the term's start, I frequently suggest—but do not require—that they each grant to their teammates a worldwide, irrevocable "license" to use the IP created during class. And—even though it may make the heads of any lawyers reading this book explode—I suggest further that an email is sufficient to grant each other this license, which likely they will never need.

What makes this license useful is that it sets expectations. By only suggesting it, I signal to students that they are consenting adults. Who am I to compel them to enter into contracts with each other or dictate what they do with their IP? To the extent I can, however, I wish to educate them *and* remain out of their disputes.

Cofounder Designation

I perennially fail to stay out of disputes between students regarding who *is* and who *is not* a cofounder of companies that emerge from entrepreneurship courses. In these classes, students typically enter independently and are then foisted on each other when compelled to assemble into teams by their instructor; in some classes, *groups* of students apply for and are granted entry. It was through that instructor-dictated teaming that I ended up in the dispute with the law student many years ago.

As an instructor, I try to prevent these disputes the same way I try to prevent disputes over IP. I tell students that they are consenting adults and that participation in the course does not create a contract between students, whether explicit or implied, regarding future activities together. Generally speaking, they are each free to go their own way without their colleagues, with all of their colleagues, or with subsets of their colleagues, as they see fit. I also tell the students about disputes that arose between student teams in previous years, again to achieve informed consent to what is about to occur in class.

I tell them what to expect of their peers: some will make excellent founders, some terrible founders, and many will lie in the middle. They are all at the start of their lives and pulled in different directions by heterogeneous aspirations, careers, romances, and other plans. Start-up teams in school are, in sum, *dynamic*. Student cofounders come and go.

I usually tell the students that they are best served by *not* creating a formal legal entity during the term and instead deferring such decisions until they are further along in their entrepreneurial journey, by which point all of their would-be team members will be in a better position to make decisions about themselves and the team. (Of course, some student founders are already well past this point by the time they join the class: they have incorporated and are already enjoying substantial business. For those start-ups, disputes over founder designations are uncommon.)

My efforts to ensure students are well-informed is not foolproof. I regularly see situations in which Bill and Nala leave Camila behind once the term ends. Typically, this is voluntary; Camila has other priorities. But occasionally, Camila is aggrieved and seeks either compensation or someone to *force* Bill and Nala to accept her as a cofounder. (Such a thing is generally not *possible* and never *practical*.) I am often the reluctant adjudicator of that dispute.

Disputes of this sort are almost always a bad sign for everyone involved. The failure of students to come to an accord on their own is evidence that they are poor negotiators and probably low on emotional intelligence.

Sometimes, student founders that split up found *competing* ventures. This is roughly the story behind ConnectU and Facebook, which were each founded at Harvard, although those companies did not emerge from a for-credit course.[36] The founders of ConnectU, which was a similar idea to Facebook, accused Mark Zuckerberg of stealing their IP when he founded Facebook. The companies settled their dispute, and ConnectU received a large sum from Facebook.

Despite my blemished track record preventing cofounder disputes, I stand by my methodology. It is not the place for the university or me to inject ourselves in the affairs of consenting adults. It is, though, my responsibility to ensure that students understand the legal complexities that might arise from participating in entrepreneurship classes.

Legal Agreements with Outside Parties

I've discussed NDA and similar legal agreements between students within a class, and I've argued that students ought not be compelled to sign them as a condition of their participation in a class. Founders who seek NDAs from their student colleagues overestimate what an NDA will accomplish. But what about NDAs with counterparties outside class?

On occasion, schools work with outside companies that provide projects for students to work on in class. This can be wonderful. Faculty who want students to have a rich educational experience— which ought to be *all* of us—are eager to incorporate "real-world" content into our classes. (We're also often grateful to have a third party design and supply some of the work for the semester.)

This arrangement, however, can be complicated by attached "strings." For example, I was once approached by a fast-growing start-up, founded by one of our alumni, that wanted to explore new markets and thought such practical "customer discovery" experience would fit nicely in an entrepreneurship class. The company wanted me to sign an NDA, and that was fine for *me*. But the company also wanted students to sign NDAs as well as IP assignments that would grant the company ownership to the students' work products. That, for me, was too much.

It is understandable for companies to ask for NDAs so they feel comfortable sharing data and resources without the risk that their private information is leaked. Indeed, NDAs and IP agreements are the *norm* in corporate research partnerships. Absent an NDA, a company might understandably be reticent to share data it considers private with students. One could argue, therefore, that these NDA and IP assignments have the benefit of making projects even more realistic to the students, and that without data sharing, such educational opportunities available to students are surely diminished.

I agree with that assertion. Yet as I implied above, I don't think such agreements are appropriate in university classes. It is too much of an encroachment of corporate norms into the university. Universities are fundamentally about open inquiry and dialogue—the *dissemination* of knowledge, not its concealment (see chapter 7).

Furthermore, such agreements create a legal risk for students. In chapter 2, I described the need for universities to use a stringent level of informed consent in their own agreements with students, and I think the same standard applies here. Do students understand the liability they are incurring when signing up for a class that requires some legal agreements?

As I also discussed in chapter 2, a part of informed consent is having reasonable outside alternatives to an agreement. Imagine a degree program in which a course is *required* and students in that course are obligated to sign legal agreements with an outside company. What is a student to do if they require this course for graduation, but are unwilling to enter into such agreements?

The easiest solution in this case is, I think, to eschew legal agreements with outside parties when possible. Certainly in *research*, this is often not possible; faculty are working at the fore of knowledge and cannot advance without corporate engagement predicated on legal agreements between the university, its faculty, and the corporate partner.

It's difficult to believe that *teaching* is not possible without such agreements. Nevertheless, when a class simply cannot occur without legal agreements from students, those students should have plausible alternatives—a way to get the similar educational benefits that does not require a legal agreement with an outside party. For instance, that could be a "canned" project or independent study with faculty.

Liability and Risk

One aspect of legal complexity I have trouble precluding concerns the liabilities that student entrepreneurs encounter because of their commercial activities. I believe this is unique to entrepreneurship courses. It is difficult to imagine any *legal* risk to which a student in Ancient Greek 101 is exposed by submitting a paper. In contrast, student entrepreneurs are often involved in commerce: buying, selling, promising, contracting, and other commercial, liability-generating activities.

In chapter 5, I described the legal liabilities incurred by student founders, mostly focused on liabilities created by legally questionable activities, including violating a student's immigration status, operating an illegal food business, or otherwise violating the law. Student founders will also have liabilities created by *completely aboveboard* activities. For example, a student selling widgets incurs product liability from those sales. What if a child chokes on a widget the student sells? A student providing cloud-based software-as-a-service databases to customers, however informally, incurs the liability of losing those customers' data. An on-campus drone sandwich delivery start-up can go wrong in innumerable ways.

Of course, it's fine if students take those risks on their own. The problem for educators is that we ask them to take those risks for a grade in a class. Indeed, the students who have the most successful start-ups—the ones usually getting the highest grades and doing the most "business"—are those incurring the most liability. (Putting aside the earlier discussion of these project grades being problematic because they are frequently poor indicators of an individual student's mastery of the course material, here I'm describing what *actually* rather than what *should* happen in class.)

Clearly, most businesspersons insulate themselves from the legal liabilities of their companies using corporate legal structures. Founders in the United States, for instance, will create a "limited liability corporation," which has the effect its name advertises, or a C corporation, which acts similarly, or some other less common option. Corporate and liability law is different in other countries. Still, most student founders are early enough in their start-up journeys that they have not yet wrapped themselves in such corporate veils—which means that they are incurring personal legal liability. Indeed, as I said earlier, I advise students not to incorporate because they are so early in their journeys that it doesn't make sense; for example, they barely know their cofounders and don't have a proven business model. But without a legal veil, the students in my classes incur legal liabilities through their commercial activities.

This is not typically a problem, and I don't want to make too much of it, but it is the truth. It is important that students be aware of the legal liability they might accrue in entrepreneurship courses and give their informed consent.

Diversity, Equity, Inclusion, and Belonging

I want to end this chapter discussing *diversity, equity, inclusion, and belonging* (DEIB).

Entrepreneurship, alas, is far from a diverse, inclusive vocation. This is manifest concretely in the funding dollars flowing to founders. Multiple studies show that although women of color comprise roughly a fifth of the US population, they receive less than 1 percent of venture capital funding in the United States.[37] By some counts, women-led start-ups receive just 2 percent of funding in the United States, despite the fact that women are roughly *half* the population, and Black founders receive about 1.4 percent of venture capital funding.[38]

Entrepreneurship's lack of diversity is also manifest in how US news and popular media portray founders. Do a web search for images of "entrepreneur" and your screen will be wall-to-wall white men.

What are underrepresented students to make of this? Entrepreneurship is, with some probability, a path to great wealth, and with certainty, a grand adventure rich with nonpecuniary rewards. How terrible for a student to see these grim statistics and think "entrepreneurship is not for me," "I am not welcome here," or "the barriers are too great." What a loss.

As educators, I think we have a threefold obligation here. First, we must show the world as it is. That requires that we not shy away from grim statistics but instead address them head-on. Sunlight, it is said, is the best disinfectant. Students should understand the antecedents of the sad situation these statistics convey, including the long-term, structural discrimination by which underrepresented persons are denied participation in social networks, access to capital, and ultimately participation in entrepreneurship.[39] They should also understand the efficacy of efforts to increase representation in entrepreneurship and adjacent areas, such as science, technology, engineering, and medicine.[40]

The second obligation of educators is to show the world as it ought to be. Above all, this means featuring protagonists whose distribution hews not to the distribution of extant entrepreneurs but rather to the population writ large. To do otherwise is, I think, a tacit endorsement of the status quo. In contrast, one must seek out underrepresented founders to be in-class guests, competition judges, and case protagonists. Doing so requires, for me at least, reaching outside my homophilous network. Each year, that takes a good amount of work on my part, but it is a small price to pay for students to see diverse protagonists—for underrepresented students to see themselves in the entrepreneurs and investors I chose to exalt in class, and overrepresented students to see persons who look dissimilar to them.

The final obligation is the most general and obvious: entrepreneurship educators must ensure that all students have equal opportunity at a university regardless of their race, ethnicity, nationality, original, gender, sexual orientation, age, physical abilities, or religion.

Universities fail in this last regard in many ways, as we do as individual educators. Here's a short tale of one of my own failures.

Like most educators, I know DEIB is important. I do my utmost to bring diverse speakers to campus. I also highlight the diversity of our own student body. If we have a panel of student speakers, a group student lunch with an illustrious alum, or a public relations photo of student founders, I try to make sure that is a diverse group of student founders. This, though, can have perverse consequences.

Years ago, I knew a woman named Ellie who was a student and the founder of a tech-heavy venture. Women are classically underrepresented in tech ventures, and so I found every opportunity I could to highlight Ellie's work. I invited her to meet with donors, pitch in contests, and appear in our annual report. After one such invitation, a colleague confided in me that Ellie did not want to do all of these things, but felt compelled to do so when I asked. I had created work for Ellie based on her gender—work that I didn't ask of other students. This is often called the "minority tax," meaning a situation wherein underrepresented persons are asked to do tasks that others are not.[41] Frequently, these are uncompensated or "nonpromotable" tasks.[42]

Since my experience with Ellie, I am more mindful of the requests I make of students. Indeed, I think it's fair to say I apply a high level of scrutiny to my requests of and suggestions to students. I now rarely ask individual students for their participation in extracurricular events. Instead, I offer broad solicitations. I make sure those solicitations are seen by students in classes, clubs, and other student affinity groups I know to be diverse.

Recommendations:

- Give grades that represent your best estimate of a student's SMC, without including things unrelated to that competence, such as attending class, coming to office hours, asking questions, or trying hard.

- Use instruments that give you an accurate measurement of a student's SMC. Certain instruments are good at developing student's competence, and other instruments are good at measuring it—but *they're not the same.* In particular, group projects in entrepreneurship classes are good instruments for developing student competence in entrepreneurship, but bad ones for measuring an individual student's competence, especially if the grading of that project is outsourced to investors or other guest judges.

- Explicitly obtain students' informed consent for project-based entrepreneurship classes premised on students having an understanding at the start of the term of their legal risks and legal rights, particularly with respect to IP and their (non)status as cofounders of ventures begun in class.

- Do not appropriate students' IP for personal use or on behalf of the university (see chapter 2).

- In for-credit classes, keep information about students (as likely required by FERPA in the United States) confidential *and* about their ventures—even if that hampers efforts to connect students with investors.

- Be wary of requiring students to sign legal agreements with outside companies as a condition for enrollment in a class. When such agreements are unavoidable, ensure students have a plausible alternative.

- Feature diverse protagonists, entrepreneurs, and investors at your school. Ensure all students have the opportunity to partake in entrepreneurship. Be mindful of the minority tax and burdens placed on the underrepresented.

7
Should We Even Be Teaching Entrepreneurship?

Having come this far in the book and read of so many challenges, one might reasonably ask whether entrepreneurship should even be taught in universities. As I am paid to teach entrepreneurship and spent my career in the field, you will perhaps not be surprised to find that I think the answer is yes, but that opinion is not universal. Even less universal is the opinion that entrepreneurship *can* be taught.

As an incoming lecturer at Yale, I recall attending a barbecue in a professor's backyard. There I met a few of my new faculty colleagues from the humanities, in disciplines such as English, history, and philosophy. They spoke eloquently of current affairs, academia, and their latest books. When the conversation turned to me, I sheepishly announced that I would be teaching entrepreneurship.

I might as well have said arc welding or plumbing. They were not impressed. How, one probed, was that a scholarly endeavor? What could you possibly *teach* about entrepreneurship? How would students nourish their minds with such thin intellectual gruel?

How Did Entrepreneurship Enter the College Curriculum?

For much of Yale's history, entrepreneurship likely would not have been an acceptable topic of study. We are a *liberal arts* university that prizes the general over the specific, the scholarly over the vocational. This vision of a liberal education was famously articulated in a three-part report issued by the faculty and corporation of Yale in 1828; it has "been reprinted several times in excerpted form and quoted extensively and commented upon by many scholars in the standard works on the history of American higher education."[1] The most well-known excerpt from what is generally known as the Yale Report of 1828 is the following:

> The two great points to be gained in intellectual culture, are the discipline and the furniture of the mind; expanding its powers, and storing it with knowledge. . . . A commanding object, therefore, in a collegiate course, should be, to call into daily and vigorous exercise the faculties of the student. Those branches of study should be prescribed, and those modes of instruction adopted, which are best calculated to teach the art of fixing the attention, directing the train of thought, analyzing a subject proposed for investigation; following, with accurate discrimination, the course of argument; balancing nicely the evidence presented to the judgment; awakening, elevating, and controlling the imagination; arranging, with skill, the treasures which memory gathers; rousing and guiding the powers of genius. All this is not to be effected by a light and hasty course of study; by reading a few books, hearing a few lectures, and spending some months at a literary institution.[2]

The report argued for a departure from the status quo: rather than focus on cultivating character, discipline, and piety in young citizens of the US aristocracy (then almost all white men), the purpose of a university education would be to expand the mind. This opened the door for a departure from the classical curriculum.

Yale, though, chose not to walk through the very door the report had opened, siding with the status quo with respect to the kinds of study that would expand the mind's powers. Latin and ancient Greek were in; professional courses were out. "Our object," the report stated, "is not to teach that which is peculiar to any one of the professions; but to lay the foundation which is common to them all."[3]

The report's broad view of education proved prescient. The same cannot be said of the report's adherence to the "dead languages" along with traditional eighteenth-century mores and modes of education.

Other universities were not so timid. "In the 1820s," wrote one education historian, "many began to sense this apparent dichotomy between the moral/public thrust of traditional liberal education as taught through the classical curriculum and the requirements and needs of an entrepreneurial society."[4] No longer would education be the domain of a privileged few seeking a traditional education in the classics. In the democratic "entrepreneurial society" of the United States, university education became increasingly available to those outside the "aristocracy" (even if still largely white and male for another century) who wanted not piety but instead *utility*.

"During the ten years after 1865," as another education historian wrote, "almost every visible change in the pattern of American higher education lay in the direction of concessions to the utilitarian type of demand for reform."[5] Those concessions came swiftly.

In 1866, Ezra Cornell wrote that he would "found an institution where any person could find instruction in any study," and the inaugural president of Cornell's namesake university elaborated that "four years of good study in one direction are held equal to four years of good study in another."[6] In 1868, the incoming president of Princeton University extolled utility and bemoaned its absence:

> Do you not see the terrible risk of wearying and disgusting the mind, when it is making its first and most hopeful efforts, and giving it ever after, by the laws of mental association, a distaste for severe studies? True, the exercise of the mind, like that of the body, is its own reward; but both are most apt to be undertaken when there is some otherwise pleasant or profitable object in view. . . . If after we have walked so hard we see and find nothing of value, if we are required to labor for that which profiteth not, to fight as one that beateth the air, the issue is not likely to be refreshing and give life and hope, but ennui and unconquerable aversion to exertion. I hold that

> every study should, as far as possible, leave not a distaste but a relish
> on the palate of the young, so that they may be inclined to return
> to it.[7]

The door the Yale Report had opened and then, in essence, quickly shut was opened again four decades later—this time to stay. No longer were the so-called dead languages the sin qua non of an educated mind. Universities and courses of study began to diversify. David Starr Jordan, president of Stanford University, declared that the entire university movement "is toward reality and practicality."[8]

By the 1900s, elective courses in more "practical" disciplines, such as the sciences and engineering, were commonplace.[9] Even studying *business* at the university level became acceptable; in 1881, Joseph Wharton endowed what later became the Wharton School at the University of Pennsylvania, and Harvard Business School opened in 1908. Yale did not follow suit; so conservative was Yale around the time of the Harvard Business School founding that Harvard's president, Charles Eliot, wrote, "The manners & customs of the Yale Faculty are those of a porcupine on the defensive. The other colleges were astonished at first, but now they just laugh."[10]

My school, the Yale School of Management, did not open until 1976, and even then was opposed by a few lingering porcupines.[11] When I first joined the Yale School of Management, the most senior, soon-to-retire professor told me that for some faculty at Yale (but not the management school), the rule was, "If you can make money at it, we won't teach it." He was only half joking. Fortunately, that view is now rare. History has, I think, spoken. The prevailing view today is that one's mind can be sharpened on many different "rocks," through many different courses of study—and that these rocks can include practical courses of study such as engineering, business, and even entrepreneurship.

As the founder of Princeton's Institute for Advanced Study, most famous as the academic home of Albert Einstein for the last twenty years of his life, wrote in 1930, "That business is a phenomenon of major importance is undeniable; that, therefore, it behooves universities interested in phenomena and in problems to study the phenomena and problems of business is clear."[12] I certainly agree. That is not to say that entrepreneurship is *better* than other disciplines or that an education in which one studies entrepreneurship exclusively would be a *good* education. It is to say merely that entrepreneurship is an appropriate component of a university education.

Does Entrepreneurship Fit with University Missions?

Furthermore, entrepreneurship seems wholly consistent with the missions of most modern universities. Yale's mission, for instance, includes "improving the world today and for future generations through outstanding research and scholarship, education, preservation, and practice."[13]

Part of the mission of the University of Michigan is "to serve the people of Michigan and the world through preeminence in creating, communicating, preserving and applying knowledge, art and academic values."[14]

The mission of Cambridge University in England includes "to contribute to society through the pursuit of education, learning, and research at the highest international levels of excellence."[15]

MIT's mission involves "generating, disseminating, and preserving knowledge, and to working with others to bring this knowledge to bear on the world's great challenges."[16]

Many university missions also express the objective of "expanding" the minds of students by filling them with knowledge. Stanford University's founding grant envisions "a university with such seminaries of learning as shall make it of the highest grade, including . . . the studies and exercises directed to the cultivation and enlargement of the mind; Its object, to qualify its students for personal success, and direct usefulness in life."[17]

"Direct usefulness in life" is known as an *instrumental* benefit; "enlargement of the mind" is an *intrinsic* benefit; the distinction between these two types of benefits is both common and ancient.[18] Knowledge is among the relatively small number of *goods* that are generally considered to have intrinsic value; they include, for example, consciousness, love, pleasure, and health.[19] Universities that espouse a liberal arts education emphasize the intrinsic benefit—that knowledge is a good for its own sake and not for other outcomes it produces in life.[20] In other words, if you believe knowledge has intrinsic value, it is presumed you would choose a life with more knowledge over any other life, all else being equal.

It's hard to see any reason why entrepreneurship education wouldn't fit comfortably into the missions of these universities. The instrumental benefits of entrepreneurship education seem obvious. And if we accept that "four years of good study in one direction are held equal to four years of good study in another," as the first Cornell president wrote, there's no reason to think the study of entrepreneurship is impoverished of intrinsic benefits like other fields of study. Of course, that depends on there *being* entrepreneurship knowledge.

Is There Entrepreneurship "Knowledge"?

In the branch of philosophy concerned with the *theory* of knowledge, which is known as epistemology, knowledge is often understood as *justified true belief* (this is not the only way of formalizing the concept of knowledge, and of course, is not universally agreed on).[21] Thus for Jane to know some fact X, it is necessary and sufficient that Jane believes X; X is true (one cannot *know* that which is false); and Jane's belief in X is *justified*.

The nature of Jane's justification for her belief can take a few forms. Perhaps she has substantial evidence that X is true (called the *evidentialist* account), or maybe her belief is produced by a reliable cognitive mechanism, such as firsthand sensory experience (called the *reliablist* account). It doesn't matter here; for our purposes, it's enough that you accept that knowledge requires some justification.

Why is justification needed? Consider the situation in which you hide a ball behind your back in one of your hands. If I firmly *believe* that the ball resides in your left hand and that is *true*, it would be incorrect to say that I have *knowledge* of the ball's location. No, it was a lucky guess.

Using this formal account, does *entrepreneurship knowledge* (justified true belief) exist, and is it possible to create it in students? Sure. Consider, for example, an empirical finding from academic research that in the United States, the more racially diverse a community, the more it benefits from venture capital investments.[22] This proposition is easily communicated, understood, and justified (by sound study design and research methods), and is a piece of entrepreneurship knowledge, little different than the multitude of other knowledge typically absorbed by students in a university, such as the names of sonnets written by William Shakespeare, the shape of π orbitals in ethylene, or the relationship between tariffs and deadweight loss in economics.

Conditional on being both true and justified, nothing about propositions related to entrepreneurship seems different from propositions in other subjects and hence would support the notion that entrepreneurship knowledge cannot be created in students.

Of course, it might be that entrepreneurship is relatively "weak" as a field of scholarly inquiry. Why? Depending on the parameters set for "scholarly inquiry," one might argue that entrepreneurship knowledge is in shorter supply or more poorly justified than knowledge in other fields. Entrepreneurship is certainly a complex, messy social phenomenon in which rigorous empirical study is challenging at best—as is often the case for studies in the sociology realm. Conducting randomized, controlled trials in entrepreneurship seems difficult compared to how the same might be done in the natural

sciences or even in, say, a discipline such as development economics. Plus the subjects of such studies can prove particularly opaque
to researchers: small, private start-ups in the entrepreneurship ecosystem flit into and out of existence, and therefore are less amenable to study than large, public corporations.

No wonder that entrepreneurship is frequently perceived as a
weak discipline in schools of management and entrepreneurship
scholars—at least through certain lenses—and lumped in with other
scholars in diverse "strategy" groups that include all the management faculty who don't quite fit into other groups. My academic
colleagues in well-established management disciplines such as economics, finance, and organizational behavior often muse about how
difficult it is to identify a canonical body of thought differentiating
entrepreneurship from these other fields of study and research.[23]
My academic colleagues in disciplines outside business schools—
and particularly in the humanities—can be downright dismissive.

Of course, entrepreneurship scholars have less trouble seeing the
measures and bounds of our field.[24] They rightly point out that entrepreneurship research has become more rigorous and even easier as
the phenomenon of entrepreneurship along with its supporting
industries such as venture capital have matured and proliferated in
recent decades.[25] In short, there weren't many start-ups decades
ago, now there are more, and scholars have gotten better at studying them, despite the messy experimental challenges. Thus our
knowledge about entrepreneurship—and as educators, we are in the
business of creating such knowledge—is growing in both quantity
and quality. With that grows our justified true belief.

Entrepreneurship education differs greatly from one university
to another, encompassing many different methods and goals.[26] Irrespective of those differences, though, I think it's fair to say that all
institutions truly engaged in educating students intend that those
students acquire knowledge.

To the extent that entrepreneurship educators teach propositions that are true and we better justify those propositions, we do our job well. Of course, if we teach propositions with uncertain veracity or ones that are poorly justified, we do our job poorly. Such is often the case when teaching relies heavily on anecdotes and war stories, which are more prone to the distortions of hindsight, fundamental attribution error, and other cognitive biases. But poor teaching is just that; it can happen in any discipline and has nothing to do with entrepreneurship in particular.

This brings us to another question: If, as I think I've made clear, entrepreneurship knowledge *does* exist, *can it actually be taught—* that is, *is entrepreneurship teachable*? You may wonder why that is a question worth exploring. The answer lies partially in a question from antiquity and partially in the dismissive attitude of all of those entrepreneurs who argue that it is completely learned in practice.

Is Entrepreneurship Teachable?

To set the stage, let's return to Plato, who first made an appearance in chapter 5. In the opening lines of his dialogue *Meno*, the title character poses a series of questions that we need to answer for entrepreneurship, even having established that there is entrepreneurship knowledge. Meno asks Socrates,

> Can you tell me, Socrates—is virtue something that can be taught?
> Or does it come by practice? Or is it neither teaching nor practice
> that gives it to a man but natural aptitude or something else?[27]

It should be noted that the Greek word here translated as "virtue"—ἀρετή (*aretē*)—is somewhat different than what we think of as virtue in modern usage, with its moral overtones. In ancient Greek, the word also means "excellence," and it signifies a central ideal in the culture ranging from desirable human characteristics, such as being a good leader of people, to admirable qualities in nonhuman things, like the sharpness of a good knife. But it is not specifically virtue in either its ancient or modern meaning that concerns us here; rather, it is the question about *teaching* something so, well, *ephemeral*. Let's pose Meno's questions again, slightly revised and substituting "entrepreneurship" for "virtue":

> Is entrepreneurship something that can be taught? Or does it come by practice? Is it some sort of *natural* aptitude that some possess and that cannot be acquired by those who do not?

The many founders who feel that entrepreneurship is best learned through practice—through *being* a founder and *doing* entrepreneurship—contend that their most indelible lessons were learned through the "school of hard knocks," and that the prospect of learning lessons like those in a classroom are laughable. These skeptics reject the notion of entrepreneurship as *teachable*—and make a compelling argument. Look at how many of the most famous founders, such as Gates and Zuckerberg, *dropped out* of school. Not only is university education not helpful to founders, some say, but it can even hold you back.

If that is true, it's a doozy of an ethical dilemma for entrepreneurship educators: if entrepreneurship *cannot* be taught, are we duping students by taking their tuition and delivering snake oil in return, claiming to teach the unteachable? We could even ask whether it's possible that we actually *harm* students by teaching them entrepreneurship. Should we worry that through entrepreneurship education, "young people are exhorted to embark on risky, opportunistic or socially irresponsible careers," or are "exploited as unwitting tools of economic development," as one academic author cautioned during the dot-com bubble?[28]

To sort this all out, let's take a deeper dive into the teachability of entrepreneurship and try to answer the first of Meno's questions. Could the skeptics be correct?

Entrepreneurship would not be teachable if, for instance, knowledge about entrepreneurship simply didn't exist, or if it does exist but is somehow not transmissible in the classroom. This might be the case if entrepreneurship knowledge comprises not facts and propositions but rather know-how—that is, some kind of ineffable skill that can be acquired only through entrepreneurial experience. (Know-how and how it is imparted were raised in chapters 4 and 6; I discuss it further below.) Or it might simply be that you can learn all you want about entrepreneurship, but it won't matter a lick unless you've got certain personality traits—some sort of entrepreneurship *areté* (the *nature* argument, also explored below).

I think I've made it quite clear that knowledge about entrepreneurship *does* exist, and it's the sort of knowledge that *can be* taught. Admittedly, though, I doubt most people who are skeptical of entrepreneurship's teachability attribute that to there being *no* knowledge (facts) to impart, but rather that the kind of knowledge one acquires in a classroom is not what makes for good entrepreneurs. We could teach propositions and facts about entrepreneurship all day long, they might insist, yet that it wouldn't make our students better entrepreneurs. Similarly, as I wrote in chapter 6, I could teach you all about physics, how gears work, how to maintain and build a bike, the technique of pedaling and turning, and so on, but having done all that, it would be wrong to say that you know how to ride a bike.

This is a more plausible critique of entrepreneurship education than the one that entrepreneurship education lacks scholarly knowledge. It draws on the idea that there are different forms of knowledge—and corresponds to Meno's second question to Socrates regarding whether virtue came about by practice.

Where Do Entrepreneurship Know-how and Practice Fit In?

I introduced Ryle, an epistemologist, in chapter 6, along with his famous 1945 address to the Aristotelian Society in which he argued that all forms of knowledge are not alike, distinguishing between what he and other so-called anti-intellectualists call *knowledge-how* (or know-how) and *knowledge-that*.[29] The latter is propositional knowledge such as "maxims, imperatives, regulative propositions, prescriptions, canons, recipes, rules, theories."[30] For example, I *know that* customer lifetime value ought to exceed the cost of customer acquisition for a successful app; I also *know how* to ride a bike and (at least based on my track record) build a successful tech company.

It's easy to articulate knowledge-that, or propositional knowledge, and transfer it through testimony; know-how, not so much.[31] Rather than simply transferring it, know-how—because it is some kind of ineffable, practical capacity to excel at something, as the argument goes—can be acquired only through practice.[32]

Ryle's know-how is not entirely original; it is quite similar to Aristotle's concept of τέχνη (*tékhnê*), one of three types of knowledge Aristotle articulated (I touched on this in chapter 4).

To Aristotle, tékhnê was—as this excellent definition from the *Dictionary of Philosophy* spells out—"the set of principles, or rational method, involved in the production of an object or the accomplishment of an end; the knowledge of such principles or method; art." Aristotle distinguished it from ἐπιστήμη (*epistēmē*), which is basically scientific knowledge and from which our word "epistemology" comes; and φρόνησῐς (*phrónēsis*), which refers to practical wisdom. Tékhnê resembles epistēmē, continues the *Dictionary of Philosophy*, "in implying knowledge of principles, but differs in that its aim is making or doing, not disinterested understanding."[33]

Put another way, tékhnê is the knowledge associated with making things and bringing new things into being. In the case of entrepreneurship, what is brought into being is a company, nonprofit, product, or vision.

I quoted Aristotle's view on the tékhnê type of knowledge in chapter 4, and it's worth noting again that he did not see it as something one could acquire through lectures and reading books:

> We learn an art or craft by doing the things that we shall have to do when we have learnt it: for instance, men become builders by building houses, harpers by playing on the harp.[34]

In this view, entrepreneurs become better entrepreneurs by being entrepreneurs—through practice to acquire know-how or tékhnê. To fill a student's head with the kind of propositional knowledge one mostly acquires in a classroom is therefore folly; excellence comes from practice, not study.

If that is true, and excellence follows from know-how and know-how results from practice, the university will be limited in what it can do for would-be entrepreneurs. It is simply not possible for any university to offer students the depth of entrepreneurship practice that student founders would get working on their ventures full time. Even semi-immersive experiences such as summer accelerators and leaves of absence to work on one's start-up are imperfect imitations of the "real-world" experience of entrepreneurship—and not only because they likely continue to include some sort of "safety net."

To be honest, the empirical literature largely upholds this perspective; many studies show that entrepreneurship education is *correlated* with entrepreneurial success *and* an increase in campus start-up activity.[35] Most studies of entrepreneurship education and its relationship with entrepreneurial success fail, however, to tell us whether entrepreneurship education makes students better entrepreneurs or it's just that students who are innately good entrepreneurs are choosing to take entrepreneurship classes. In other words, most studies do not show *causality*. Why is that? These studies are replete with limitations, not the least of which is that few involve actual entrepreneurship students. They also rarely, if ever, employ what constitutes the very substance of research in so many other disciplines, but that is nearly impossible in entrepreneurship: randomized controlled trials, natural experiments, or quasiexperiments. That means there are rarely clear, *attributable* results.

That said, there have been a few studies that use such designs. In a meta-analysis of those studies, the authors find that most human capital interventions, such as mentoring and nondegree education, do *nothing* to make entrepreneurs more successful; the effects of these interventions are not statistically significant, lending credence to the view that entrepreneurship is not teachable.[36] Most of the studies reviewed, though, were of entrepreneurs in a broad sense—so broad that it basically could include most anyone who is self-employed. The studies were not specifically of entrepreneurs like those top-tier universities typically produce—and they were definitely not of students.

A handful of other studies not in that review have conflicting results, showing a causal, positive relationship between entrepreneurship education and entrepreneurial success. For instance, there's the randomized control trial that tested the efficacy of the popular "lean start-up" or "evidence-based entrepreneurship" approach over a yearlong period, and found that teams of entrepreneurs who were taught evidence-based entrepreneurship were more likely to pivot and less likely to close up shop.[37] Clearly, that's a short time horizon, and merely staying afloat is a not a particularly aspirational outcome—but at least it shows that entrepreneurship education can have some effect, even if modest.

Another study examined the fates of start-ups accepted and "almost accepted" to accelerator programs, using a so-called regression discontinuity design—which takes advantage of a cutoff, such as the accepted/not-accepted cutoff for an incubator based on some kind of quantitative scoring—to help more clearly see the effects of the programs they examined.[38] It's more apparent because the start-ups on either side of the cutoff are so similar to each other before the incubator program begins; in fact, they're almost the same. This group of researchers found that the accelerator programs increased venture success.

Again, neither of these two studies looked at university-based entrepreneurs—students—or university classes in entrepreneurship, but both show that interventions to help entrepreneurs are at a minimum not futile; start-ups can be nudged toward success. Notably, the ventures studied in both examples have relatively high human capital and therefore might be similar to the kinds of ventures that emerge from top-tier universities.

Admittedly—and this is the bottom line—no study of which I am aware shows *specifically* that university entrepreneurship education increases entrepreneurial success. The best-designed empirical studies on entrepreneurship interventions are about entrepreneurship education only in part, and focus on practice. They show that many—and perhaps most—interventions have no effect on entrepreneurial outcomes, and those that do involve a lot of practice, not the acquisition of propositional knowledge or book learning.

This brief report on research doesn't mean we should abandon all of our entrepreneurship classes at universities. Most vocations students pursue after graduation will involve some know-how, and students will find themselves, at first, imperfectly prepared for those vocations. Does entrepreneurship involve more know-how than other vocations? Plausibly. But even if that's the case, the combination of entrepreneurship propositional knowledge, knowledge-that, with know-how could be quite beneficial. If I'm taught the physics of a bicycle's functioning, it may not mean I know how to ride a bicycle, but I am certainly no worse off for that knowledge as long as I'm not lured into a false confidence of my bike-riding ability.

Furthermore, not all students take entrepreneurship classes in order to become actual entrepreneurs; just as they may take a music class to appreciate and understand music better and become more musical—but not with the express goal of becoming a musician—students may take an entrepreneurship class to become more entrepreneurial. For such students, know-how is plausibly less consequential. This is also true for the many classes "about" entrepreneurship rather than "for" it.[39] Topics such as public policy and entrepreneurship, entrepreneurial finance, venture capital, the history of entrepreneurship, the organizational behavior of small firms, the psychology of entrepreneurship, and so on, can be of interest to students pursuing other career paths and impart a good deal of propositional knowledge. I imagine that few founders would question the teachability of public policy and entrepreneurship.

Finally, even absent proof that university entrepreneurship education specifically produces start-up success, there is strong evidence that formal education generally *does*.[40] We do know that going to college makes you a better entrepreneur; indeed, it appears that entrepreneurs get more out of college than nonentrepreneurs—including income returns to formal education that are between 2 and 13 percent higher for entrepreneurs, with particularly high returns for those who go to a prestigious university and start a venture related to their majors.[41]

That said, I prefer to think of myself as endowing student founders with knowledge rather than merely a credential from an Ivy League school.

So as it turns out, the skeptics of entrepreneurship education who believe universities cannot teach students to be more successful entrepreneurs are wrong—at least in the sense that university education generally makes students more successful entrepreneurs. Yet they are right in that the best evidence we have at the moment suggests that university entrepreneurship education is likely doing little to make students more successful entrepreneurs.

I am somewhat crestfallen by this conclusion. Do I feel like my students are better entrepreneurs for having taken my classes? Sure. But I can't possibly know whether I merely attracted to my class students predisposed to success. That brings me to the next reason skeptics raise about entrepreneurship education: the seemingly eternal *nature versus nurture* question.

What about Nature versus Nurture?

Meno also raises the age-old question of nature versus nurture. It's an easy view with which to empathize—which is certainly what the media is doing when it exalts entrepreneurs who are dropouts and iconoclasts. And it is buttressed by what seems like the "natural ability" that we see all around us in other endeavors, such as art, music, drama, and sports.

Education in art helps me understand theories and gives me tools with which to critique works of art, but it is no guarantee of professional success as an artist. It may not even make me capable of drawing more than a stick figure. Likewise, I can learn all the rules of basketball and theories behind how it is best played, but while that may increase my enjoyment of the game, no amount of classes in basketball will make me capable of competing in the NBA—which requires practice and, dare I say, some sort of natural ability. It's not an accident that while there have been a few relatively short NBA stars over the decades, "you can't teach height," as the infamous former Boston Celtics coach Red Auerbach reportedly said.

There are many analogous, desirable attributes in entrepreneurship that feel unteachable to me—grit, confidence, tolerance for risk, and so on. And there is some empirical evidence showing that there is merit to this view and at least in part, entrepreneurship is indeed nature. For example, a study of the career trajectories of Swedish children raised by adoptive parents found that those with a biological parent who was an entrepreneur were about 20 percent more likely to become an entrepreneur than those whose biological parents were not entrepreneurs.[42] That said, the adoptive parents had an even larger effect, showing that both nature (the biological parents) and nurture (the adoptive parents) matter. These results are consistent with studies of twins, which suggest (remarkably) that a nontrivial component of one's choice to become an entrepreneur can be explained by genetics.[43]

Of course, merely choosing to become an entrepreneur is a very different thing than becoming a successful one. Here too, though, nature matters. An investigation of the linkage between the cognitive abilities of youths and their later earnings as entrepreneurs found that entrepreneurs have a return on general cognitive abilities that is 30 percent higher than that of nonentrepreneurs.[44] It turns out—in the specific context of being an entrepreneur—that the old axiom that it pays to be smart in life is truer for entrepreneurs than for wage employees, at least in terms of an actual return on smarts.

How Does Meno Answer?

So what are the answers to our Meno-like questions for entrepreneurship? It turns out that there's some bit of yes to all three: entrepreneurship is learnable through teaching, learnable through practice, and innate, in parts. I find this to be an intuitive conclusion and suspect that's the case for you as well.

The fact that natural ability and practice are important to entrepreneurial success is not a reason to disregard entrepreneurship education or deem it an unworthy component of university education. Art, music, and drama are uncontroversial components of university education despite the importance of natural ability and practice in these disciplines. In all of these, students need not have explicitly vocational goals. Why should entrepreneurship—and entrepreneurship classes—be different?

That leaves one last question to consider, which I raised earlier: Is it possible that there is some harm to students in teaching them entrepreneurship.

Is Teaching Entrepreneurship Harmful?

In the early 1900s, Antarctic explorer Sir Ernest Shackleton reputedly placed the following advertisement in search of compatriots for an expedition (the provenance of the quote is suspect):

> Men wanted for hazardous journey. Low wages, bitter cold, long hours of complete darkness. Safe return doubtful. Honor and recognition in event of success.

A better solicitation would be difficult to write. It is stirring, inspirational, and accurate in its appraisal of the prospects faced by would-be adventurers. Entrepreneurship, too, comes with perils; a summary of the best empirical studies of the returns to entrepreneurship finds that the median entrepreneur works more but earns less than the median nonentrepreneur, and the lowest quartile of entrepreneurs earns substantially less than the lowest quartile of employees.[45] All the returns in entrepreneurship are captured by a handful of exceedingly successful founders—the Gates and Jobs of the world. This highly skewed distribution of returns is similar to professions such as acting and music that are characterized by "superstar" economics in which a handful of people capture an outsize fraction of the aggregate returns.[46]

In light of such facts, it is easy to see how teaching entrepreneurship could be harmful. Imagine if I instilled students with false confidence and taught them only hokey lessons from anecdotal experience, leaving them ill prepared for careers as entrepreneurs. That is surely harm; such teaching robs students of autonomy by forcing them to make decisions based on false or incomplete information. Receiving such teaching, my students may wade recklessly into entrepreneurship, forgoing other opportunities that might benefit them more.

I have a professional and moral obligation to ensure my students enter entrepreneurship (or not) with clear eyes, aware of what awaits them: "Low wages, bitter cold, long hours of complete darkness. . . . Honor and recognition in event of success."

Epilogue

Is there a better job on campus than teaching entrepreneurship? It's difficult to imagine. Entrepreneurship educators are in the enviable position of seeing the university's boldest students—the dreamers, the do-ers, and sometimes the downright delusional. These students come from all over campus and work on all manner of ventures, from heartwarming nonprofits to scalable tech ventures potentially worth billions of dollars. What a privilege to be in the service of these students, stand beside them at the inception of their ventures, delight in their successes, and console them in their failures.

If the role of entrepreneurship educator is rewarding, it is in equal measure challenging. It is so in no small part because of the numerous ethical dilemmas faced by entrepreneurship educators. Should educators be investors in their students? Do lifestyle ventures deserve the same support as high-tech ones on campus? I discussed dozens of such questions in this book.

These questions arise due to a confluence of factors. Chief among those is the reality that students do not merely study entrepreneurship but often are actual entrepreneurs while in school. The practice of entrepreneurship necessarily leads student founders into many activities, relationships, and conundrums with which students in other disciplines are not burdened. Into this mix is layered the potential for fame, fortune, and other ends desired by students, faculty, and universities alike.

An Overdue Reckoning

In reading through these chapters, you have probably figured out that the factors that give rise to the ethical complications and perils of campus entrepreneurship and those that make campus entrepreneurship wondrous and magical are, for the most part, the very same.

To make our ethical dilemmas disappear altogether would require neutering campus entrepreneurship, rendering it the domain of abstract study rather than engaged practice. Doing so is not only impossible—*that* genie is already out of the bottle—but also madness, as it would leave the university abased and diminished. And so if we are to have campus entrepreneurship, we are left with its ethical dilemmas and must deal with them.

In many ways, this situation is analogous to that of college sports, which are rife with ethical problems—including the financial exploitation of student athletes and shambolic veneer of an education some student athletes receive. As Derek Bok, the former president of Harvard, wrote,

> What can intercollegiate sports teach us about the hazards of commercialization? First of all, the saga of big-time athletics reveals that American universities, despite their lofty ideals, are not above sacrificing academic values—even values as basic as admissions standards and the integrity of their courses—in order to make money. Nor will they shrink from exploiting their own students, where necessary, to succeed on the playing field.[1]

Entrepreneurship is not immune from these risks. Campus sports and campus entrepreneurship both call into question the relationship between the university and student as well as the very purpose of the university itself. As a *New Yorker* writer asked in 2013 about Stanford University, "Is [it] still a university? . . . The school now looks like a giant tech incubator with a football team."[2]

Fortunately, universities are beginning to acknowledge and address the ethical perils of campus sports.[3] I believe a similar reckoning is brewing in entrepreneurship education.

An Apology

Nietzsche asserted, "To the preachers of morals . . . I give this advice: if you want eventually to deprive the best things and situations of all their worth, then keep talking about them the way you have been!"[4] I have tried herein to sketch for you the beginning of the reckoning I think is due in entrepreneurship education. I hope that I have done so without depriving entrepreneurship of even a single ounce of its worth.

I make no claim to be a great entrepreneurship educator, nor to hew without error to the prescriptions in this book—although I try to keep those prescriptions in my mind and follow them as best I can. My approach—both in these pages and my practice as an educator—rests largely on deontological theories such as Kant's ethics, role ethics, and professional ethics. Relying on these theories, I often spoke in the preceding chapters about educators' duties to students and our fiduciary relationship to student founders, which binds us to act in students' best interests. I find this manner of thinking most helpful in managing the complex ethical landscape of entrepreneurship education.

I've found so-called act consequentialist thinking to be more tricky. That's the version of consequentialism that requires me to foresee the consequences of every choice I make to determine which is most ethical. Act consequentialism is exhausting, to be frank, and at least for me is too easily perverted by my latent self-interest and biases. Perhaps like me, you also can justify almost anything you want to if you put your mind to it.

The deontological approach is easier, and I suspect—in a convenient twist—it has the best consequences too: if we do our duty to student founders and act as their fiduciaries, it will be, in the end, better for both those founders and the university. (This makes my line of thinking somewhat akin to "rule consequentialism.")

I recognize that some of my stances may seem puritanical and will surely not apply wholesale to other educators lives as they apply to mine. I am in one of the more bleached parapets of the ivory tower. Though we may differ on the margin, I hope I've kindled your interest in the central question of this book: What does it mean to be a *good* entrepreneurship educator? For me in my work, and perhaps for you in yours, it is profoundly important to answer that question. It reminds me of what Socrates says early in Plato's *Republic*, as he and his interlocutors begin to address the question of "whether the just also live better than the unjust and are happier." Socrates notes that "the argument is not just about any question, but about the way one should live."[5]

For us, the question is about the way one should *teach*.

Surely being a good entrepreneurship educator means to have taught students theory and helped them put that theory into practice. But just as surely, it must mean, as I contended here, to have done right by one's students and put each student *first* (insomuch as such a thing is possible), so that in the end, one acted in students' best interests when profit and pedagogy came into conflict. Every educator so doing makes their campus a better place for student entrepreneurs.

With this in mind, allow me to sketch the prefiguring vision of a campus on which entrepreneurship educators embrace the rich ethical challenges of their jobs. With apologies to John Winthrop—whose 1630 sermon to the people of the Massachusetts Bay Colony produced the enduring notion of erecting "a city upon a hill," something "all people" will look up to—I give you the campus upon a hill—an ideal I think all educators can look up to.[6]

The Idealized Campus

What does an idealized, entrepreneurship-friendly campus look like? It is a campus on which student founders are first and foremost *students*. They are not potential lucrative investments, success stories to extol on social media, or future wealthy donors. They are just students to whom the university owes an education and in whose best interest the university acts.

As for this university, it prioritizes education over acceleration. It is unacquisitive. It eschews investing in student founders, wary of the moral hazards and conflicts of interest doing so creates. Instead, it strives to create a campus on which private investors are welcome so that student founders can easily find capital, and vice versa. What acceleration the idealized university *does* offer is offered in moderation and with circumspection.

Epictetus wrote, "Every individual is strengthened and preserved by acting in keeping with himself—a builder by building, a grammarian by doing grammar."[7] At our idealized institution, entrepreneurship educators *educate*. These educators are keen to avoid role conflicts that would call their commitment to students into question. They are not consultants, shadow founders, or investors.

The idealized university includes both scholars and practitioner educators. The scholars understand the importance of practice, and the practitioners recognize the importance of scholarship. The practitioners bring their experiences into the classroom, but they do so in a scholarly fashion, not telling war stories, but using their lived experience to help students understand how the theory of entrepreneurship is manifest in practice. These practitioners subjugate their outside activities to their teaching, not abiding conflicts or the appearance thereof.

Educators at our idealized university love entrepreneurship, but they are not Pollyannaish about it. They understand that entrepreneurship is not the right choice for many students or perhaps even most. So these educators are not disappointed in students who make other choices. They are content that students receive an education in entrepreneurship, thereby becoming *entrepreneurial*—if not entrepreneurs per se.

To those students who do pursue entrepreneurial endeavors, these educators offer encouragement but never false hope or undue pressure. Some students will choose lifestyle ventures, nonprofits, and other forms outside the archetypal high-tech, high-growth venture—and that is fine at our campus on a hill. Such students are not discouraged from their dreams, but neither are they misled about the difficulty of their tasks.

Educators at our idealized institution are trustworthy confidants for student founders. The student asks, "Can I trust you?"; the answer is an unambiguous yes. Students share their "dirty laundry," and the educators keep students' secrets. Everyone recognizes that this comes at a cost; these educators are not and cannot be salespeople for student ventures. While they freely grant students' requests for introductions to investors and other service providers, these introductions always stop short of being recommendations or endorsements, in either direction. Students are left to tell their own stories, particularly with investors. In other words, student founders on our idealized campus are not handed fish but instead taught how to fish. At all times, educators seek to disintermediate themselves; they aspire to not be in the business of connecting students to service providers but rather to create and foster an environment in which these parties can easily find each other.

The campus on a hill reflects a high standard—one that may never be met fully by any university. It's not a standard I've achieved, but my colleagues and I are making progress year by year. We have many chances to practice, and for that, I am grateful.

Practice was, to Aristotle, *the* mechanism by which we develop virtue and ethical wisdom. He wrote that "we become just by doing just acts, temperate by doing temperate acts, brave by doing brave acts." Our virtue, he said, is "made perfect by habit."[8]

How wonderful, then, for entrepreneurship educators to have so many opportunities for practice. Aristotle's predecessor Heraclitus famously said that we never step in the same river twice. Similarly, no matter how long you've been teaching, no educator teaches the same class twice, for you're not the same person, and it's not the same class. Each semester is a clean slate, with different students and a different self. It is a chance to excel, be better versions of ourselves, better serve student entrepreneurs, and more skillfully greet the numerous ethical quandaries arising in entrepreneurship education.

Notes

Preface

1. Thomson, "The Trolley Problem."

2. Hume, *Dialogues concerning Natural Religion*, 142.

Chapter 1

1. Bok, *Universities in the Marketplace.*

2. Boettiger and Bennett, "Bayh-Dole."

3. Brooks et al., "Entrepreneurship in American Higher Education," 6.

4. Torrance, "Entrepreneurial Campuses"; Morris and Liguori, "Preface," xiv.

5. Morris and Liguori, "Preface."

6. Lange, "The Innovation Campus"; Markman et al., "Entrepreneurship and University-Based Technology Transfer"; Croce, Grilli, and Murtinu, "Venture Capital Enters Academia."

7. Henrekson and Johansson, "Gazelles as Job Creators"; Carree and Thurik, "The Impact of Entrepreneurship on Economic Growth," 578; Parker, *The Economics of Entrepreneurship*, 264; Van Praag and Versloot, "The Economic Benefits and Costs of Entrepreneurship."

8. Åstebro and Tåg, "Gross, Net, and New Job Creation by Entrepreneurs," 79; Parker, *The Economics of Entrepreneurship*, 265.

9. Benz, "Entrepreneurship as a Non-Profit-Seeking Activity," 30.

10. Schumpeter, *The Theory of Economic Development*, 9.

11. McMullen and Shepherd, "Entrepreneurial Action."

12. Schumpeter, *Capitalism, Socialism, and Democracy*, 93.

13. Acs, Audretsch, and Lehmann, "The Knowledge Spillover Theory of Entrepreneurship."

14. Brooks et al., "Entrepreneurship in American Higher Education," 14.

15. Kierkegaard, *Either/Or*, 116.

16. Ruef, "Entrepreneurial Groups."

17. Steiner, "Not Just the What and How."

18. Lee and Wong, "Entrepreneurship Education"; Morris and Liguori, "Preface," xvii.

19. Merton, "The Role-Set," 110.

20. Meyers, "Professional Ethics."

21. Homer, *The Odyssey*, book 21, line 370.

22. Kierkegaard, *A Kierkegaard Anthology*, 194.

Chapter 2

1. de Sales, *Oeuvres Complètes*.

2. Meyers, "Professional Ethics," 1; Bayles, *Professional Ethics*.

3. Almond, "Reasonable Partiality in Professional Relationships."

4. "Code of Medical Ethics"; "Model Rules of Professional Conduct."

5. National Education Association, "Code of Ethics for Educators." See also Cholbi, "Ethical Issues in Teaching."

6. Schuwerk, "The Law Professor as Fiduciary."

7. Weeks and Haglund, "Fiduciary Duties of College and University Faculty and Administrators."

8. Quoted in Sullivan, *An Introduction to Kant's Ethics*, 65.

9. Kant, *Groundwork of the Metaphysics of Morals*, GR 4:392, 193; Paton, "The Aim and Structure of Kant's *Grundlegung*."

10. Kant, *Groundwork of the Metaphysics of Morals*, GR 4:421, 222.

11. Kant, *Groundwork of the Metaphysics of Morals*, GR 4:429, 230.

12. Atwell, *Ends and Principles in Kant's Moral Thoughts*.

13. Laukkanen, "Exploring Alternative Approaches in High-Level Entrepreneurship Education," 42.

14. Bix, "Consent and Contracts"; Bullock, "Valid Consent."

15. Bullock, "Valid Consent."

16. Bix, "Consent and Contracts," 3.

17. Feld, *Venture Deals*, ch. 8.

18. Rubin, "Implementing and Enforcing Online Terms of Use"; Reed, *Entrepreneurship Law*.

19. Reed, *Entrepreneurship Law*, 298.

20. Eisenmann, *Why Startups Fail*.

21. Mulcahy, "6 Myths about Venture Capitalists"; Metrick and Yasuda, *Venture Capital and the Finance of Innovation*, 62.

22. Bok, *Universities in the Marketplace*, ch. 3.

23. Cohen et al., "The Design and Evaluation of Startup Accelerators."

24. Da Rin, Hellmann, and Puri, "A Survey of Venture Capital Research," 625.

25. Da Rin, Hellmann, and Puri, "A Survey of Venture Capital Research"; Kaplan and Schoar, "Private Equity Performance"; Robinson and Sensoy, "Cyclicality, Performance Measurement, and Cash Flow Liquidity in Private Equity."

26. Nanda, Samila, and Sorenson, "The Persistent Effect of Initial Success."

27. Lerner, *Boulevard of Broken Dreams*, 119; Dahaj and Cozzarin, "Government Venture Capital and Cross-Border Investment"; Fini et al., "Complements or Substitutes?"

28. Hutchins, *The Higher Learning in America*, 69.

Chapter 3

1. Gillett, "A Wharton Professor Reveals 'The Worst Financial Decision' He Ever Made."

2. Parker, *The Economics of Entrepreneurship*, 156.

3. Lauto, Salvador, and Visintin, "For What They Are, Not for What They Bring," 4.

4. Allen and Gale, *Comparing Financial Systems*.

5. Hardgrave, "Professors Invest in Student Startups."

6. Aulet, "What I Have Learned about Teaching Entrepreneurship," 3.

7. Baril, "The Ethical Importance of Roles," 725; Hardimon, "Role Obligations," 334.

8. Swanton, "Virtue Ethics, Role Ethics, and Business Ethics."

9. Dare and Swanton, *Perspectives in Role Ethics*.

10. Andre, "Role Morality as a Complex Instance of Ordinary Morality"; Johnson, *The Role Ethics of Epictetus*, 8.

11. Hardimon, "Role Obligations," 337.

12. Merton, "The Role-Set."

13. Getzels and Guba, "Role, Role Conflict, and Effectiveness," 165.

14. Andre, "Role Morality as a Complex Instance of Ordinary Morality," 75.

15. Kitchener, "Dual Role Relationships," 218.

16. Biaggio, Paget, and Chenoweth, "A Model for Ethical Management of Faculty, 184.

17. Hardgrave, "Professors Invest in Student Startups."

18. Kitchener, "Dual Role Relationships," 218

19. Blevins-Knabe, "The Ethics of Dual Relationships in Higher Education," 154.

20. Thompson, "Stanford and Its Startups."

21. Blevins-Knabe, "The Ethics of Dual Relationships in Higher Education," 154.

22. La Fontaine, *Original Fables*, 57.

23. Demosthenes, *The Public Orations of Demosthenes*, 111.

24. Blevins-Knabe, "The Ethics of Dual Relationships in Higher Education," 153.

25. Bentham, *An Introduction to the Principles of Morals and Legislation*, 1.

26. Bowring, *The Works of Jeremy Bentham*, 142.

27. John Stuart Mill, *Utilitarianism*, 13.

28. McCormack, "The Sexual Harassment of Students by Teachers," 29.

29. Williams, *Moral Luck*, 20–39; Nagel, *Mortal Questions*, 31–32.

30. Kitchener, "Dual Role Relationships," 220.

31. Blevins-Knabe, "The Ethics of Dual Relationships in Higher Education," 161.

32. Quoted in Hadot, *The Inner Citadel*, 134.

Chapter 4

1. Duranton and Puga, "Micro-Foundations of Urban Agglomeration Economies"; Porter, "Clusters and the New Economics of Competition."

2. Gompers et al., "How Do Venture Capitalists Make Decisions?," 186.

3. Erb, "How a Ghostwriter Makes $200,000 a Year."

4. Smith, "Origin and Uses of *Primum Non Nocere*."

5. Veysey, *The Emergence of the American University*, 3.

6. Kaplan, "Voluntary Support of Education."

7. "Major Private Gifts to Higher Education."

8. Parker, *The Economics of Entrepreneurship*, 416.

9. Feld, "I Got My Bathroom."

10. Epictetus, *Discourses*, 161.

11. Wasserman, *The Founder's Dilemmas*, 69.

12. Bennis and O'Toole, "How Business Schools Lost Their Way," 100, 102.

13. Small, "The Transmission of Skill," 102.

14. Aristotle, *Nicomachean Ethics*, II.i.4.

15. Sidgwick, *The Methods of Ethics*, 318.

16. Sanchez-Burks et al., "Mentoring in Startup Ecosystems," 8; Eisenberg, *Incomplete Contracts*.

17. Bazelon, "The Stanford Undergraduate and the Mentor."

18. Sun et al., "Stanford Doesn't Trust Joe Lonsdale to Mentor Students."

19. Bazelon, "The Lessons of Stanford's Sex-Assault-Case Reversal."

20. Shane, "Why Hiring Non-Academics to Teach Entrepreneurship Is a Bad Idea."

21. Hargreaves, "The Emotional Practice of Teaching."

22. Bennis and O'Toole, "How Business Schools Lost Their Way," 98.

23. Schoemaker, "The Future Challenges of Business," 119.

Chapter 5

1. "Mission and History."

2. Siegel, Siegel, and Macmillan, "Characteristics Distinguishing High-Growth Ventures."

3. Lerner and Malmiender, "With a Little Help from My (Random) Friends."

4. Azoulay et al., "Age and High-Growth Entrepreneurship."

5. Munier, "Schumpeterian Entrepreneur."

6. Kirzner, "The Alert and Creative Entrepreneur," 148.

7. Henrekson and Johansson, "Gazelles as Job Creators."

8. Kessler, "The Food-Sharing Economy Is Delicious and Illegal."

9. Morris, "Can You Start a Business on a Student Visa?"

10. Mead, "Legal and Regulatory Issues Governing Cannabis."

11. Isaac, "How Uber Deceives the Authorities Worldwide."

12. Coldwell, "Airbnb's Legal Troubles."

13. Howell, Niessner, and Yermack, "Initial Coin Offerings."

14. Asay et al., *Family Violence from a Global Perspective*, 48.

15. Parker, "Brendan Kennedy."

16. Chiu et al., "Public Health Impacts to Date."

17. Nutt, King, and Nichols, "Effects of Schedule I Drug Laws."

18. King, "Letter from Birmingham Jail."

19. Henley, "Uber Clashes with Regulators in Cities around the World."

20. Plato, *Crito*, 50b.

21. Plato, *Crito*, 50d.

22. Agostino et al., "Rule of Law and Regulatory Quality as Drivers of Entrepreneurship."

23. Cudd and Eftekhari, "Contractarianism."

24. Narveson, *The Libertarian Idea*, 148.

25. Hobbes, *Leviathan*, 99.

26. Bix, "Consent and Contracts"; Bullock, "Valid Consent."

27. Regis, "What Is Ethical Egoism?"

28. Kierkegaard, *The Journals of Søren Kierkegaard*, 15.

29. Bodie, "Employment as Fiduciary Relationship."

30. Aaron, "Employees' Duty of Loyalty," 144, 143.

31. Freeland, "Social and Legal Bases of Managerial Authority," 198.

32. Tolentino, "Promise of Vaping and the Rise of JUUL."

33. McDonald, "Ethereum Emissions."

34. Dreier et al., "Free-to-Play"; Galekovic, "It Costs $110,000 to Fully Gear-Up in Diablo Immortal."

35. Lambert et al., "Taking a One-Week Break from Social Media."

36. Bartoletti et al., "Dissecting Ponzi Schemes on Ethereum."

37. Kata, "A Postmodern Pandora's Box"; Mathew et al., "Hate Begets Hate."

38. Carreyrou, *Bad Blood*.

39. Jensen et al., "Entrepreneurs and the Truth," 127.

40. Jensen et al., "Entrepreneurs and the Truth," 127.

41. Veysey, *The Emergence of the American University*, 21.

42. Boyle, "Goodbye, Trolley Problem"; "4 Strategies."

43. JUUL Labs, "Adam and James' Thesis Presentation."

44. Steinbauer et al., "Conflicting Drivers of Entrepreneurial Ethics"; Crane, "Ethics, Entrepreneurs and Corporate Managers."

45. Jensen et al., "Entrepreneurs and the Truth," 131.

46. Smith, *The Theory of Moral Sentiments*, ch. 5.

Chapter 6

1. Blumberg, *Startup CEO*.

2. Smallwood, *An Historical Study of Examinations and Grading Systems*, 42, 51.

3. Veysey, *The Emergence of the American University*, 57.

4. Cahn, *Saints and Scamps*, 26; Gullickson, "Student Evaluation Standards," 214; Brighouse, "Grade inflation and Grade Variation," 74.

5. Close, "Fair Grades," 380.

6. Chartier, "Truth-Telling," 39.

7. Close, "Fair Grades," 370.

8. Bullock, "Valid Consent."

9. Close, "Fair Grades," 382.

10. Gullickson, "Student Evaluation Standards," 214.

11. Chartier, "Truth-Telling," 49.

12. Weis, "Grading," 10.

13. Chartier, "Truth-Telling," 53.

14. Ryle, "Knowing How and Knowing That"; Small, "The Transmission of Skill," 92.

15. Small, "The Transmission of Skill," 102.

16. Ewens and Townsend, "Are Early Stage Investors Biased against Women?"; Lee and Huang, "Gender Bias."

17. Brooks et al., "Investors Prefer Entrepreneurial Ventures Pitched by Attractive Men."

18. Chartier, "Truth-Telling," 61, 62.

19. Ramirez, *FERPA Clear and Simple*.

20. Ramirez, *FERPA Clear and Simple*, 25.

21. Jensen et al., "Entrepreneurs and the Truth."

22. Barron and Green, "Accidental Founders," 87, 92

23. Barron and Green, "Accidental Founders," 87.

24. Burgmer, Forstmann, and Stavrova, "Ideas Are Cheap"; Schrage, *The Innovator's Hypothesis*, 17.

25. Morrison, *Biotechnology Law*, 36.

26. Oikonomides, "Records," 75

27. Dadpey, "Issues Enforcing Nondisclosure Agreements"; Garfield, "Promises of Silence."

28. Quoted in Chereminsky and Gillman, *Free Speech on Campus*, 59.

29. Katz, Harshman, and Dean, "Nondisclosure Agreements in the Classroom," 248.

30. Reinhardt, introduction, xvi.

31. Silvernagel, Olson, and Stupnisky. "Mine, Yours, or Ours?," 211.

32. Wright and Katz, "Protecting Student Intellectual Property," 158; Macfarlane. "Re-Framing Student Academic Freedom," 728.

33. Wright and Katz, "Protecting Student Intellectual Property," 158.

34. "Defending the Freedom to Innovate."

35. Gattari, "Determining Inventorship."

36. Newkirk and Viehauser, "The ConnectU and Facebook Dispute."

37. "Quick Facts"; Girlboss, "The Venture Capital World Has a Problem with Women of Color."

38. Bittner and Lau, "Women-Led Startups"; Braswell, "Black Founders."

39. Ahl, "Why Research on Women Entrepreneurs Needs New Directions."

40. Ozkazanc-Pan and Muntean, "Networking Towards (In)equality."

41. Rodríguez, Campbell, and Pololi, "Addressing Disparities in Academic Medicine."

42. Babcock et al., "Gender Differences."

Chapter 7

1. Herbst, "The Yale Report of 1828," 213.

2. Yale College, "Report of the Faculty."

3. Yale College, "Report of the Faculty."

4. Lane, "The Yale Report of 1828 and Liberal Education," 330.

5. Veysey, *The Emergence of the American University*, 60.

6. Cornell, "Ezra Cornell, Letter to Andrew Dickson White"; quoted in Veysey, *The Emergence of the American University*, 84.

7. M'Cosh, "Inauguration Address," 18.

8. Veysey, *The Emergence of the American University*, 60.

9. Veysey, *The Emergence of the American University*, 118.

10. Quoted in Veysey, *The Emergence of the American University*, 50.

11. Donaldson and Weber, *Entrepreneurial Leader*, ch. 7.

12. Flexner, *Universities*, 165.

13. Lassila, "Mission Control."

14. https://president.umich.edu/about/mission.

15. https://www.cam.ac.uk/about-the-university/how-the-university-and-colleges-work/the-universitys-mission-and-core-values.

16. https://policies.mit.edu/policies-procedures/10-institute/11-mission-and-objectives.

17. https://web.stanford.edu/dept/registrar/bulletin1112/4792.htm.

18. Jones, "Why Do We Value Knowledge?"

19. Pritchard, "Knowledge and Final Value."

20. Nussbaum, "Education for Profit, Education for Freedom."

21. Steup, "Epistemology"; Ichikawa and Steup, "The Analysis of Knowledge"; Dutant, "The Legend of the Justified True Belief Analysis"; Kaplan, "It's Not What You Know That Counts"; Gettier, "Is Justified True Belief Knowledge?"

22. Samila, and Sorenson, "Community and Capital in Entrepreneurship and Economic Growth."

23. Croci, "Is Entrepreneurship a Discipline?," 4.

24. Landström, "The Evolution of Entrepreneurship as a Scholarly Field"; Shane and Venkataraman, "The Promise of Entrepreneurship as a Field."

25. Mollick, *The Unicorn's Shadow*.

26. Mwasalwiba, "Entrepreneurship Education"; Middleton and Donnellon, "Personalizing Entrepreneurial Learning," 167.

27. Plato, *Meno*, 70a.

28. Laukkanen, "Exploring Alternative Approaches in High-Level Entrepreneurship Education," 42.

29. Ryle, "Knowing How and Knowing That"; Fantl, "Knowledge How."

30. Small, "The Transmission of Skill," 92.

31. Poston, "Know How to Transmit Knowledge?"

32. Small, "The Transmission of Skill," 102.

33. Morrow, "Techne."

34. Aristotle, *Nicomachean Ethics*, II.i.4.

35. Martin, McNally, and Kay, "Examining the Formation of Human Capital in Entrepreneurship."

36. Hogendoorn et al., "The Effects of Human Capital Interventions on Entrepreneurial Performance.""

37. Camuffo et al., "A Scientific Approach to Entrepreneurial Decision Making."

38. Hallen, Cohen, and Bingham, "Do Accelerators Work?"

39. Haase and Lautenschläger, "The 'Teachability Dilemma' of Entrepreneurship."

40. Hogendoorn et al., "The Effects of Human Capital Interventions on Entrepreneurial Performance," 805; Van Der Sluis, Van Praag, and Vijverberg, "Education and Entrepreneurship Selection and Performance," 796.

41. Van Praag, Witteloostuijn, and Van Der Sluis, "The Higher Returns to Formal Education for Entrepreneurs versus Employees"; Åstebro, Bazzazian, and Braguinsky, "Startups by Recent University Graduates and Their Faculty," 668.

42. Lindquist, Sol, and Van Praag, "Why Do Entrepreneurial Parents Have Entrepreneurial Children?"

43. Nicolaou and Shane, "Entrepreneurship and Occupational Choice."

44. Hartog, Van Praag, and Van Der Sluis, "If You Are So Smart, Why Aren't You an Entrepreneur?"

45. Åstebro, "The Returns to Entrepreneurship."

46. Rosen, "The Economics of Superstars."

Epilogue

1. Bok, *Universities in the Marketplace*, 54.

2. Thompson, "The End of Stanford?"

3. Dees, Cianfrone, and Andrew, "Show Me the Money!"

4. Nietzsche, *The Gay Science*, 166.

5. Plato, *Republic*, 352d.

6. Winthrop, "A Model of Christian Charity."

7. Epictetus, *Discourses*, 158–159.

8. Aristotle, *Nicomachean Ethics*, II.i.4–5, II.i.3.

Bibliography

Aaron, Benjamin. "Employees' Duty of Loyalty: Introduction and Overview." *Comparative Labor Law and Policy Journal* 20, no. 2 (Winter 1999): 143–154.

Acs, Zoltan J., David B. Audretsch, and Erik E. Lehmann. "The Knowledge Spillover Theory of Entrepreneurship." *Small Business Economics* 41, no. 4 (2013): 757–774.

Adams, Marcus P. "Empirical Evidence and the Knowledge-That/Knowledge-How Distinction." *Synthese* 170 (2009): 97–114.

Agostino, Mariarosaria, Annamaria Nifo, Francesco Trivieri, and Gaetano Vecchione. "Rule of Law and Regulatory Quality as Drivers of Entrepreneurship." *Regional Studies* 54, no. 6 (2020): 814–826.

Ahl, Helene. "Why Research on Women Entrepreneurs Needs New Directions." *Entrepreneurship Theory and Practice* 30, no. 5 (2006): 595–621.

Allen, Franklin, and Douglas Gale. *Comparing Financial Systems.* Cambridge, MA: MIT Press, 2001.

Almond, Brenda. "Reasonable Partiality in Professional Relationships." *Ethical Theory and Moral Practice* 8, no. 1 (2005): 155–168.

Andre, Judith. "Role Morality as a Complex Instance of Ordinary Morality." *American Philosophical Quarterly* 28, no. 1 (1991): 73–80.

Aristotle. *Nicomachean Ethics.* Translated by H. Rackham. Cambridge, MA: Harvard University Press, 1926.

Asay, Sylvia M., John DeFrain, Marcee Metzger, and Bob Moyer, eds. *Family Violence from a Global Perspective: A Strengths-Based Approach.* Newbury Park, CA: SAGE Publishing, 2013.

Åstebro, Thomas. "The Returns to Entrepreneurship." In *The Oxford Handbook of Entrepreneurial Finance*, edited by Douglas Cumming. New York: Oxford University Press, 2012.

Åstebro, Thomas, Navid Bazzazian, and Serguey Braguinsky. "Startups by Recent University Graduates and Their Faculty: Implications for University Entrepreneurship Policy." *Research Policy* 41, no. 4 (2012): 663–677.

Åstebro, Thomas, and Joacim Tåg. "Gross, Net, and New Job Creation by Entrepreneurs." *Journal of Business Venturing Insights* 8 (2017): 64–70.

Atwell, John E. *Ends and Principles in Kant's Moral Thoughts*. Vol. 22. Berlin: Springer, 1986.

Aulet, Bill. "What I Have Learned about Teaching Entrepreneurship: Perspectives of Five Master Educators." In *Annals of Entrepreneurship Education and Pedagogy—2018*, edited by Charles H. Matthews and Eric W. Liguori. Cheltenham, UK: Edward Elgar Publishing, 2018.

Azoulay, Pierre, Benjamin F. Jones, J. Daniel Kim, and Javier Miranda. "Age and High-Growth Entrepreneurship." *American Economic Review: Insights* 2, no. 1 (2020): 65–82.

Babcock, Linda, Maria P. Recalde, Lise Vesterlund, and Laurie Weingart. "Gender Differences in Accepting and Receiving Requests for Tasks with Low Promotability." *American Economic Review* 107, no. 3 (March 2017): 714–747.

Baril, Anne. "The Ethical Importance of Roles." *Journal of Value Inquiry* 50, no. 4 (2016): 721–734.

Barron, Esther, and Darren Green. "Accidental Founders: The Race from Class Project to Start-up." *Stanford Journal of Law, Business and Finance* 25, no. 1 (2020): 86–130.

Bartoletti, Massimo, Salvatore Carta, Tiziana Cimoli, and Roberto Saia. "Dissecting Ponzi Schemes on Ethereum: Identification, Analysis, and Impact." *Future Generation Computer Systems* 102 (2020): 259–277.

Bayles, Michael D. *Professional Ethics*. Belmont, CA: Wadsworth Publishing, 1988.

Bazelon, Emily. "The Lessons of Stanford's Sex-Assault-Case Reversal." *New York Times Sunday Magazine*, November 4, 2015.

Bazelon, Emily. "The Stanford Undergraduate and the Mentor." *New York Times Sunday Magazine*, February 11, 2015.

Beamon, Krystal K. "'Used Goods': Former African American College Student-Athletes' Perception of Exploitation by Division I Universities." *Journal of Negro Education* (2008): 352–364.

Bennis, Warren G., and James O'Toole. "How Business Schools Lost Their Way." *Harvard Business Review* 83, no. 5 (May 2005): 96–104.

Bentham, Jeremy. *An Introduction to the Principles of Morals and Legislation.* Oxford: Clarendon Press, 1879.

Benz, Matthias. "Entrepreneurship as a Non-Profit-Seeking Activity." *International Entrepreneurship and Management Journal* 5, no. 1 (2009): 23–44.

Biaggio, Maryka, Tana Lucic Paget, and M. Sue Chenoweth. "A Model for Ethical Management of Faculty—Student Dual Relationships." *Professional Psychology: Research and Practice* 28, no. 2 (1997): 184–189.

Bittner, Ashley, and Brigette Lau. "Women-Led Startups Received Just 2.3% of VC Funding in 2020." *Harvard Business Review*, February 25, 2021.

Bix, Brian. "Consent and Contracts." In *The Routledge Handbook of the Ethics of Consent*, edited by Andreas Schaber and Peter Müller. New York: Routledge, 2018.

Blevins-Knabe, Belinda. "The Ethics of Dual Relationships in Higher Education." *Ethics and Behavior* 2, no. 3 (1992): 151–163.

Blumberg, Matt. *Startup CEO: A Field Guide to Scaling Up Your Business.* New York: John Wiley and Sons, 2020.

Bodie, Matthew T. "Employment as Fiduciary Relationship." *Georgetown Law Review* 105 (2016): 819.

Boettiger, Sara, and Alan B. Bennett. "Bayh-Dole: If We Knew Then What We Know Now." *Nature Biotechnology* 24, no. 3 (2006): 320–323.

Bok, Derek. *Universities in the Marketplace: The Commercialization of Higher Education.* Princeton, NJ: Princeton University Press, 2003.

Bowring, John. *The Works of Jeremy Bentham.* London: Simpkin, Marshall, and Company, 1843.

Boyle, Katherine. "Goodbye, Trolley Problem. This Is Silicon Valley's New Ethics Test." *Washington Post*, February 5, 2019.

Braswell, Porter. "Black Founders Only Receive 1.4% VC Funds—Here's How to Change That." *Fast Company*, August 9, 2022. https://www.fastcompany.com/90777034/black-founders-only-receive-1-4-vc-funds-heres-how-to-change-that.

Brighouse, Harry. "Grade Inflation and Grade Variation: What's All the Fuss About." In *Grade Inflation: Academic Standards in Higher Education*, edited by Lester H. Hunt. New York: SUNY Press, 2008.

Brooks, Alison Wood, Laura Huang, Sarah Wood Kearney, and Fiona E. Murray. "Investors Prefer Entrepreneurial Ventures Pitched by Attractive Men." *Proceedings of the National Academy of Sciences* 111, no. 12 (2014): 4427–4431.

Brooks, Rodney, William Scott Green, R. Glenn Hubbard, Dipak C. Jain, Linda Katehi, George McLendon, James Plummer, Myron Roomkin, and Richard Newton. "Entrepreneurship in American Higher Education." *SSRN Electronic Journal* (2007). https://papers.ssrn.com/sol3/papers.cfm?abstract_id=1291290.

Bullock, Emma C. "Valid Consent." In *The Routledge Handbook of the Ethics of Consent*, edited by Andreas Schaber and Peter Müller. New York: Routledge, 2018.

Burgmer, Pascal, Matthias Forstmann, and Olga Stavrova. "Ideas Are Cheap: When and Why Adults Value Labor over Ideas." *Journal of Experimental Psychology: General* 148, no. 5 (2019): 824–844.

Cahn, Steven. *Saints and Scamps: Ethics in Academia.* Lanham, MD: Rowman and Littlefield Publishers, 2010.

Camuffo, Arnaldo, Alessandro Cordova, Alfonso Gambardella, and Chiara Spina. "A Scientific Approach to Entrepreneurial Decision Making: Evidence from a Randomized Control Trial." *Management Science* 66, no. 2 (2020): 564–586.

Carree, Martin A., and A. Roy Thurik. "The Impact of Entrepreneurship on Economic Growth." In *Handbook of Entrepreneurship Research: An Interdisciplinary Survey and Introduction*, edited by Zoltan J. Acs and David B. Audretsch. New York: Springer, 2010.

Carreyrou, John. *Bad Blood: Secrets and Lies in a Silicon Valley Startup.* New York: Knopf Doubleday Publishing Group, 2018.

Chartier, Gary. "Truth-Telling, Incommensurability, and the Ethics of Grading." *Brigham Young University Education and Law Journal* 1 (Spring 2003): 37–81.

Chereminsky, Erwin, and Howard Gillman. *Free Speech on Campus.* New Haven, CT: Yale University Press, 2017.

Chiu, Vivian, Janni Leung, Wayne Hall, Daniel Stjepanović, and Louisa Degenhardt. "Public Health Impacts to Date of the Legalisation of Medical and Recreational Cannabis Use in the USA." *Neuropharmacology* 193 (August 2021): 108610.

Cholbi, Michael. "Ethical Issues in Teaching." In *The International Encyclopedia of Ethics.* London: Wiley-Blackwell, 2013.

Close, Daryl. "Fair Grades." *Teaching Philosophy* 32, no. 4 (2009): 361–398.

"Code of Medical Ethics." American Medical Association. Accessed November 13, 2023. https://www.ama-assn.org/delivering-care/ethics/code-medical-ethics-overview.

Cohen, Susan, Daniel C. Fehder, Yael V. Hochberg, and Fiona Murray. "The Design and Evaluation of Startup Accelerators." *Research Policy* 48, no. 7 (2019): 1781–1797.

Coldwell, Will. "Airbnb's Legal Troubles: What Are the Issues?" *Guardian*, July 8, 2014.

Cornell, Ezra. "Ezra Cornell, Letter to Andrew Dickson White, Ithaca, New York, February 23, 1868." Cornell University. Accessed November 21, 2023. https://rmc .library.cornell.edu/cornell150/exhibition/found/index.html.

Crane, Frederick G. "Ethics, Entrepreneurs and Corporate Managers: A Canadian Study." *Journal of Small Business and Entrepreneurship* 22, no. 3 (2009): 267–274.

Croce, Annalisa, Luca Grilli, and Samuele Murtinu. "Venture Capital Enters Academia: An Analysis of University-Managed Funds." *Journal of Technology Transfer* 39, no. 5 (2014): 688–715.

Croci, Cassidy L. "Is Entrepreneurship a Discipline?" Bachelor's thesis, University of New Hampshire, 2016. https://scholars.unh.edu/honors/296.

Cudd, Ann, and Seena Eftekhari. "Contractarianism." In *The Stanford Encyclopedia of Philosophy*, edited by Edward N. Zalta. Winter 2021. https://plato.stanford.edu /archives/win2021/entries/contractarianism.

Dadpey, Neda. "Issues Enforcing Nondisclosure Agreements (United States)." Resource Library, Association of Corporate Council, April 7, 2017. https://www.acc.com /resource-library/issues-enforcing-nondisclosure-agreements-united-states.

D'Agostino, Fred, Gerald Gaus, and John Thrasher. "Contemporary Approaches to the Social Contract." In *The Stanford Encyclopedia of Philosophy*, edited by Edward N. Zalta. Winter 2021. https://plato.stanford.edu/archives/win2021/entries/contractarianism -contemporary.

Dahaj, Arash Soleimani, and Brian Paul Cozzarin. "Government Venture Capital and Cross-Border Investment." *Global Finance Journal* 41 (2019): 113–127.

Dare, Tim, and Christine Swanton, eds. *Perspectives in Role Ethics: Virtues, Reasons, and Obligation.* New York: Routledge, 2019.

Da Rin, Marco, Thomas Hellmann, and Manju Puri. "A Survey of Venture Capital Research." In *Handbook of the Economics of Finance*, edited by George M. Constantinides, Milton Harris, and Rene M. Stulz. Vol. 2. Amsterdam: Elsevier, 2013.

Dees, Windy, Beth Cianfrone, and Damon Andrew. "Show Me the Money! A Review of Current Issues in the New NIL Era." *Journal of Applied Sport Management* 13, no. 2 (2021): 2.

"Defending the Freedom to Innovate: Faculty Intellectual Property Rights after Stanford v. Roche." American Association of University Professors, June 2014. https:// www.aaup.org/report/defending-freedom-innovate-faculty-intellectual-property -rights-after-stanford-v-roche-0.

Demosthenes. *The Public Orations of Demosthenes.* Translated by Arthur Wallace Pickard-Cambridge. Oxford: Clarendon Press, 1912.

de Sales, François. *Oeuvres Complètes de Saint François de Sales.* Paris: Perisse frères, 1861.

Donaldson, William H., and Karl Weber. *Entrepreneurial Leader: A Lifetime of Adventures in Business, Education, and Government.* Austin, TX: Greenleaf Book Group Press, 2018.

Dreier, Michael, Klaus Wölfling, Eva Duven, Sebastián Giralt, Manfred E. Beutel, and Kai W. Müller. "Free-to-Play: About Addicted Whales, at Risk Dolphins and Healthy Minnows. Monetarization Design and Internet Gaming Disorder." *Addictive Behaviors* 64 (2017): 328–333.

Duranton, Gilles, and Diego Puga. "Micro-Foundations of Urban Agglomeration Economies." In *Handbook of Regional and Urban Economics*, edited by J. Vernon Henderson and Jacques-François Thisse. Vol. 4. Amsterdam: Elsevier, 2004.

Dutant, Julien. "The Legend of the Justified True Belief Analysis." *Philosophical Perspectives* 29, no. 1 (2015): 95–145.

Eisenberg, Melvin A. *Incomplete Contracts.* Vol. 1. Oxford: Oxford University Press, 2018.

Eisenmann, Tom. *Why Startups Fail: A New Roadmap for Entrepreneurial Success.* New York: Currency, 2021.

Epictetus. *Discourses.* In *The Complete Works: Handbook, Discourses, and Fragments*, edited and translated by Robin Waterfield. Chicago: University of Chicago Press, 2022.

Erb, Jordan Parker. "How a Ghostwriter Makes $200,000 a Year Crafting Tweets for Superstar VCs." *Business Insider*, October 12, 2022. https://www.businessinsider.com/ghostwriter-makes-200000-a-year-crafting-tweets-for-top-vcs-2022-10.

Ewens, Michael, and Richard R. Townsend. "Are Early Stage Investors Biased against Women?" *Journal of Financial Economics* 135, no. 3 (2020): 653–677.

Fantl, Jeremy. "Knowledge How." In *The Stanford Encyclopedia of Philosophy*, edited by Edward N. Zalta. Fall 2017. https://plato.stanford.edu/archives/fall2017/entries/knowledge-how.

Feld, Brad. "I Got My Bathroom." January 25, 2008. https://feld.com/archives/2008/01/i-got-my-bathroom.

Feld, Brad. *Venture Deals: Be Smarter than Your Lawyer and Venture Capitalist.* New York: John Wiley and Sons, 2019.

Fini, Riccardo, Rosa Grimaldi, Simone Santoni, and Maurizio Sobrero. "Complements or Substitutes? The Role of Universities and Local Context in Supporting the Creation of Academic Spin-offs." *Research Policy* 40, no. 8 (2011): 1113–1127.

Flexner, Abraham. *Universities: American, English, German.* Oxford: Oxford University Press, 1930.

"4 Strategies to Integrate Ethics into Entrepreneurship Education." VentureWell, July 14, 2019. https://venturewell.org/integrate-ethics/.

Frankena, William K. *Ethics.* Englewood Cliffs, NJ: Prentice Hall, 1973.

Freeland, Robert F. "The Social and Legal Bases of Managerial Authority." *Entreprises et Histoire* 57 (2009): 194–217, 4265–4266.

Galekovic, Filip. "It Costs $110,000 to Fully Gear-Up in Diablo Immortal." *GameRant,* June 4, 2022. https://gamerant.com/diablo-immortal-pay-to-win-legendary-gems.

Garfield, Alan E. "Promises of Silence: Contract Law and Freedom of Speech." *Cornell Law Review* 83 (1997): 261.

Gattari, Patrick G. "Determining Inventorship for US Patent Applications." *Intellectual Property and Technology Law Journal* 17, no. 5 (2005): 16–19.

Gettier, Edmund L. "Is Justified True Belief Knowledge?" *Analysis* 23, no. 6 (1963): 121–123.

Getzels, Jacob W., and Egon G. Guba. "Role, Role Conflict, and Effectiveness: An Empirical Study." *American Sociological Review* 19, no. 2 (1954): 164–175.

Gillett, Rachel. "A Wharton Professor Reveals 'The Worst Financial Decision' He Ever Made—And Why It Taught Him about Success." *Business Insider,* March 2, 2016.

Girlboss. "The Venture Capital World Has a Problem with Women of Color." Accessed November 20, 2023. https://girlboss.com/blogs/read/venture-capital-woc-women-of-color.

Gompers, Paul A., Will Gornall, Steven N. Kaplan, and Ilya A. Strebulaev. "How Do Venture Capitalists Make Decisions?" *Journal of Financial Economics* 135, no. 1 (2020): 169–190.

Gullickson, Arlen R. "Student Evaluation Standards: A Paradigm Shift for the Evaluation of Students." *Prospects* 35, no. 2 (2005): 213–227.

Haase, Heiko, and Arndt Lautenschläger. "The 'Teachability Dilemma' of Entrepreneurship." *International Entrepreneurship and Management Journal* 7, no. 2 (2011): 145–162.

Hadot, Pierre. *The Inner Citadel: The Meditations of Marcus Aurelius.* Translated by Michael Chase. Cambridge, MA: Harvard University Press, 2001.

Hallen, Benjamin L., Susan L. Cohen, and Christopher B. Bingham. 2020. "Do Accelerators Work? If So, How?" *Organization Science* 31, no. 2 (2020): 378–414.

Hardgrave, Kyle. "Professors Invest in Student Startups: Taking Interest in Student Ideas, Professors Are Helping Launch Students' Careers." *Daily Pennsylvanian*, March 22, 2012.

Hardimon, Michael O. "Role Obligations." *Journal of Philosophy* 91, no. 7 (1994): 333–363.

Hargreaves, Andy. "The Emotional Practice of Teaching." *Teaching and Teacher Education* 14, no. 8 (1998): 835–854.

Hartog, Joop, Mirjam Van Praag, and Justin Van Der Sluis. "If You Are So Smart, Why Aren't You an Entrepreneur? Returns to Cognitive and Social Ability: Entrepreneurs versus Employees." *Journal of Economics and Management Strategy* 19, no. 4 (2010): 947–989.

Henley, Jon. "Uber Clashes with Regulators in Cities around the World." *Guardian*, September 29, 2017.

Henrekson, Magnus, and Dan Johansson. "Gazelles as Job Creators: A Survey and Interpretation of the Evidence." *Small Business Economics* 35, no. 2 (2010): 227–244.

Herbst, Jurgen. "The Yale Report of 1828." *International Journal of the Classical Tradition* 11 (2004): 213–231.

Hobbes, Thomas. *Leviathan*. Oxford: Clarendon Press, 1909. First published in 1651.

Hogendoorn, Bram, Iryna Rud, Wim Groot, and Henriëtte Maassen van den Brink. "The Effects of Human Capital Interventions on Entrepreneurial Performance in Industrialized Countries." *Journal of Economic Surveys* 33, no. 3 (2019): 798–826.

Homer. *The Odyssey*. Translated by Robert Fagles. New York: Viking, 1996.

Howell, Sabrina T., Marina Niessner, and David Yermack. "Initial Coin Offerings: Financing Growth with Cryptocurrency Token Sales." *Review of Financial Studies* 33, no. 9 (2019): 3925–3974.

Hume, David. *Dialogues concerning Natural Religion*. London: Thomas Nelson and Sons Ltd., 1935. First published in 1779.

Hutchins, Robert Maynard. *The Higher Learning in America*. New Haven, CT: Yale University Press, 1976. First published in 1936.

Ichikawa, Jonathan Jenkins, and Matthias Steup. "The Analysis of Knowledge." In *The Stanford Encyclopedia of Philosophy*, edited by Edward N. Zalta. Summer 2018. https://plato.stanford.edu/archives/sum2018/entries/knowledge-analysis.

Isaac, Mike. "How Uber Deceives the Authorities Worldwide." *New York Times*, March 3, 2017.

Jensen, Kyle, Tom Byers, Laura Dunham, and Jon Fjeld. "Entrepreneurs and the Truth." *Harvard Business Review*, July–August 2021. https://hbr.org/2021/07/entrepreneurs-and-the-truth.

Johnson, Brian Earl. *The Role Ethics of Epictetus: Stoicism in Ordinary Life*. Plymouth, UK: Lexington Books, 2014.

Jones, Ward E. "Why Do We Value Knowledge?" *American Philosophical Quarterly* 34, no. 4 (1997): 423–439.

JUUL Labs. "Adam and James' Thesis Presentation." YouTube, February 27, 2019. https://www.youtube.com/watch?v=ZBDLqWCjsMM.

Kant, Immanuel. *Groundwork of the Metaphysics of Morals*. Translated by Arnulf Zweig. New York: Oxford University Press, 2002. First published in German in 1786.

Kaplan, Ann E. "Voluntary Support of Education (VSE)—Summary Findings 2019." Council for Advancement and Support of Education. https://store.case.org/PersonifyEbusiness/Store/Product-Details/productId/1265836826.

Kaplan, Mark. "It's Not What You Know That Counts." *Journal of Philosophy* 82, no. 7 (1985): 350–363.

Kaplan, Steven N., and Antoinette Schoar. "Private Equity Performance: Returns, Persistence, and Capital Flows." *Journal of Finance* 60, no. 4 (2005): 1791–1823.

Kata, Anna. "A Postmodern Pandora's Box: Anti-Vaccination Misinformation on the Internet." *Vaccine* 28, no. 7 (2010): 1709–1716.

Katz, Jerome A., Ellen F. Harshman, and Kathy Lund Dean. "Nondisclosure Agreements in the Classroom: A Student Entrepreneur's Refuge or Risk?" *Journal of Management Education* 24, no. 2 (2000): 234–253.

Kessler, Sarah. "The Food-Sharing Economy Is Delicious and Illegal—Will It Survive?" *Fast Company*, July 7, 2016.

Kierkegaard, Søren. *Either/Or*. Translated by Walter Lowrie. Oxford: Oxford University Press, 1944.

Kierkegaard, Søren. *The Journals of Søren Kierkegaard: A Selection*. Edited and translated by Alexander Dru. London: Oxford University Press, 1938.

Kierkegaard, Søren. *A Kierkegaard Anthology*. Edited by Robert Bretall. Princeton, NJ: Princeton University Press, 1973.

King, Martin Luther, Jr. "Letter from Birmingham Jail." *UC Davis Law Review* 26 (1992): 835. First published in 1963.

Kirzner, Israel M. "The Alert and Creative Entrepreneur: A Clarification." *Small Business Economics* 32, no. 2 (2009): 145–152.

Kitchener, Karen Strohm. "Dual Role Relationships: What Makes Them So Problematic?" *Journal of Counseling and Development* 67, no. 4 (1988): 217–221.

Kolstad, Ivar, and Arne Wiig. "Education and Entrepreneurial Success." *Small Business Economics* 44, no. 4 (2015): 783–796.

La Fontaine, Jean de. *The Original Fables of La Fontaine*. Translated by Frederick Colin Tilney. New York: E. P. Dutton and Company, 1913.

Lambert, Jeffrey, George Barnstable, Eleanor Minter, Jemima Cooper, and Desmond McEwan. "Taking a One-Week Break from Social Media Improves Well-being, Depression, and Anxiety: A Randomized Controlled Trial." *Cyberpsychology, Behavior, and Social Networking* 25, no. 5 (2022): 287–293.

Landström, Hans. "The Evolution of Entrepreneurship as a Scholarly Field." *Foundations and Trends® in Entrepreneurship* 16, no. 2 (2020): 65–243.

Lane, Jack C. "The Yale Report of 1828 and Liberal Education: A Neorepublican Manifesto." *History of Education Quarterly* 27, no. 3 (1987): 325–338.

Lange, Alexandra. "The Innovation Campus: Building Better Ideas." *New York Times*, August 4, 2016.

Lassila, Kathrin. "Mission Control: What a New Mission Statement Says about the University." *Yale Alumni Magazine*, September–October 2016. https://yalealumnimagazine.org/articles/4334-mission-control.

Laukkanen, Mauri. "Exploring Alternative Approaches in High-Level Entrepreneurship Education: Creating Micromechanisms for Endogenous Regional Growth." *Entrepreneurship and Regional Development* 12, no. 1 (2000): 25–47.

Lautenschläger, Arndt, and Heiko Haase. "The Myth of Entrepreneurship Education: Seven Arguments against Teaching Business Creation at Universities." *Journal of Entrepreneurship Education* 14 (2011): 147–161.

Lauto, Giancarlo, Elisa Salvador, and Francesca Visintin. "For What They Are, Not for What They Bring: The Signaling Value of Gender for Financial Resource Acquisition in Academic Spin-offs." *Research Policy* 51, no. 7 (September 1, 2022): 104554.

Lee, Lena, and Poh-Kam Wong. "Entrepreneurship Education—A Compendium of Related Issues." In *The Life Cycle of Entrepreneurial Ventures*, edited by Simon Parker. Boston: Springer, 2006.

Lee, Matthew, and Laura Huang. "Gender Bias, Social Impact Framing, and Evaluation of Entrepreneurial Ventures." *Organization Science* 29, no. 1 (2018): 1–16.

Lerner, Josh. *Boulevard of Broken Dreams: Why Public Efforts to Boost Entrepreneurship and Venture Capital Have Failed—and What to Do about It*. Princeton, NJ: Princeton University Press, 2009.

Lerner, Josh, and Ulrike Malmendier. "With a Little Help from My (Random) Friends: Success and Failure in Post-Business School Entrepreneurship." *Review of Financial Studies* 26, no. 10 (2013): 2411–2452.

Lindquist, Matthew J., Joeri Sol, and Mirjam Van Praag. "Why Do Entrepreneurial Parents Have Entrepreneurial Children?" *Journal of Labor Economics* 33, no. 2 (2015): 269–296.

Macfarlane, Bruce. "Re-Framing Student Academic Freedom: A Capability Perspective." *Higher Education* 63, no. 6 (2012): 719–732.

"Major Private Gifts to Higher Education." *Chronicle of Higher Education*, July 10, 2023. https://www.chronicle.com/article/Major-Private-Gifts-to-Higher/128264.

Markman, Gideon D., Phillip H. Phan, David B. Balkin, and Peter T. Gianiodis. "Entrepreneurship and University-Based Technology Transfer." *Journal of Business Venturing* 20, no. 2 (2005): 241–263.

Martin, Bruce C., Jeffrey J. McNally, and Michael J. Kay. "Examining the Formation of Human Capital in Entrepreneurship: A Meta-analysis of Entrepreneurship Education Outcomes." *Journal of Business Venturing* 28, no. 2 (2013): 211–224.

Mathew, Binny, Anurag Illendula, Punyajoy Saha, Soumya Sarkar, Pawan Goyal, and Animesh Mukherjee. 2020. "Hate Begets Hate: A Temporal Study of Hate Speech." *Proceedings of the ACM on Human-Computer Interaction* 4, no. CSCW2 (2020): 1–24.

McCormack, Arlene. "The Sexual Harassment of Students by Teachers: The Case of Students in Science." *Sex Roles* 13, no. 1 (1985): 21–32.

McDonald, Kyle. 2021. "Ethereum Emissions: A Bottom-up Estimate." Cornell University, December 7, 2022, arXiv:2112.01238. https://arxiv.org/abs/2112.01238.

McMullen, Jeffery S., and Dean A. Shepherd. "Entrepreneurial Action and the Role of Uncertainty in the Theory of the Entrepreneur." *Academy of Management Review* 31, no. 1 (2006): 132–152.

M'Cosh, Reverend Jas. "Inauguration Address." In *Inauguration of Rev. Jas. M'Cosh, D.D., LL.D, as President of Princeton College, October 27, 1868*. Princeton, NJ: Stelle and Smith, 1868.

Mead, Alice. "Legal and Regulatory Issues Governing Cannabis and Cannabis-Derived Products in the United States." *Frontiers in Plant Science* 10 (2019): 697.

Merton, Robert K. "The Role-Set: Problems in Sociological Theory." *British Journal of Sociology* 8, no. 2 (1957): 106–120.

Metrick, Andrew, and Ayako Yasuda. *Venture Capital and the Finance of Innovation.* New York: John Wiley and Sons, 2021.

Meyers, Christopher. "Professional Ethics." In *International Encyclopedia of Ethics*. Edited by David B. Resnik. New York: Wiley Online Library, 2013.

Middleton, Karen Williams, and Anne Donnellon. 2020. "Personalizing Entrepreneurial Learning: A Pedagogy for Facilitating the Know Why." *Entrepreneurship Research Journal* 4, no. 2 (2014): 167–204.

Mill, John Stuart. *Utilitarianism*. London: Routledge, 1871."Mission and History." Yale Divinity School. Accessed November 19, 2023. https://divinity.yale.edu/about-yds/mission-history.

"Model Rules of Professional Conduct." American Bar Association. Accessed November 21, 2023. https://www.americanbar.org/groups/professional_responsibility/publications/model_rules_of_professional_conduct.

Mollick, Ethan. *The Unicorn's Shadow: Combating the Dangerous Myths That Hold Back Startups, Founders, and Investors*. Philadelphia: University of Pennsylvania Press, 2020.

Morris, Anne. "Can You Start a Business on a Student Visa?" DavidsonMorris, July 19, 2023. https://www.davidsonmorris.com/tier-4-student-start-business.

Morris, Michael H., and Eric Liguori. "Preface: Teaching Reason and the Unreasonable." In *Annals of Entrepreneurship Education and Pedagogy—2016*, edited by Michael H. Morris and Eric Liguori. Cheltenham, UK: Edward Elgar Publishing, 2016.

Morrison, Alan. *Biotechnology Law: A Primer for Scientists*. New York: Columbia University Press, 2020.

Morrow, Glenn R. "Techne." In *The Dictionary of Philosophy*, edited by Dagobert D. Runes. New York: Citadel Press, 2001. First published in 1942.

Moskowitz, Tobias J., and Annette Vissing-Jørgensen. "The Returns to Entrepreneurial Investment: A Private Equity Premium Puzzle?" *American Economic Review* 92, no. 4 (2002): 745–778.

Mulcahy, Diane. "6 Myths about Venture Capitalists." *Harvard Business Review* 91, no. 5 (2013): 80–83.

Munier, Francis. 2013. "Schumpeterian Entrepreneur." In *Encyclopedia of Creativity, Invention, Innovation and Entrepreneurship*, edited by Elias G. Carayannis. New York: Springer, 2013.

Mwasalwiba, Ernest Samwel. 2010. "Entrepreneurship Education: A Review of Its Objectives, Teaching Methods, and Impact Indicators." *Education and Training* 52, no. 1 (2010): 20–47.

Nagel, Thomas. *Mortal Questions*. New York: Cambridge University Press, 1979.

Nanda, Ramana, Sampsa Samila, and Olav Sorenson. "The Persistent Effect of Initial Success: Evidence from Venture Capital." *Journal of Financial Economics* 137, no. 1 (2020): 231–248.

Narveson, Jan. *The Libertarian Idea*. Peterborough, ONT: Broadview Press, 2001.

National Education Association. "Code of Ethics for Educators." September 14, 2020. https://www.nea.org/resource-library/code-ethics-educators.

Newkirk, Christopher D., and Ashley L. Viehauser. "The ConnectU and Facebook Dispute: Has the Final Chapter Been Written?" *Intellectual Property and Technology Law Journal* 20, no. 12 (2008): 1.

Nicolaou, Nicos, and Scott Shane. "Entrepreneurship and Occupational Choice: Genetic and Environmental Influences." *Journal of Economic Behavior and Organization* 76, no. 1 (2010): 3–14.

Nietzsche, Friedrich Wilhelm. *The Gay Science: With a Prelude in German Rhymes and an Appendix of Songs*. Translated by Josefine Nauckhoff. Cambridge: Cambridge University Press, 2001. First published in 1882.

Nussbaum, Martha C. "Education for Profit, Education for Freedom." *Liberal Education* 95, no. 3 (2008): 6–13.

Nutt, David J., Leslie A. King, and David E. Nichols. "Effects of Schedule I Drug Laws on Neuroscience Research and Treatment Innovation." *Nature Reviews Neuroscience* 14, no. 8 (2013): 577–585.

Oikonomides, Al N. "Records of 'The Commandments of the Seven Wise Men' in the 3rd c. BC." *Classical Bulletin* 63, no. 3 (1987): 67.

Ozkazanc-Pan, Banu, and Susan Clark Muntean. "Networking Towards (In)equality: Women Entrepreneurs in Technology." *Gender, Work and Organization* 25, no. 4 (2018): 379–400.

Parker, Garrett. "Brendan Kennedy: The Marijuana Billionaire Who Doesn't Smoke. *Money Inc.*, January 26, 2019.

Parker, Simon C. *The Economics of Entrepreneurship*. 2nd ed. Cambridge: Cambridge University Press, 2018.

Paton, Henry James. "The Aim and Structure of Kant's *Grundlegung*." *Philosophical Quarterly* 8, no. 31 (1958): 112–130.

Plato. *Crito*. Translated by Hugh Tredennick. In *The Collected Dialogues of Plato*, edited by Edith Hamilton and Huntington Cairns. Princeton, NJ: Princeton University Press, 1961.

Plato. *Meno*. Translated by W. K. C. Guthrie. In *The Collected Dialogues of Plato*, edited by Edith Hamilton and Huntington Cairns. Princeton, NJ: Princeton University Press, 1961.

Plato. *Republic*. Translated by Allan Bloom. New York: Basic Books, 1968.

Porter, Michael E. "Clusters and the New Economics of Competition. *Harvard Business Review* 76, no. 6 (1998): 77–90.

Poston, Ted. "Know How to Transmit Knowledge?" *Noûs* 50, no. 4 (2016): 865–878.

Pritchard, Duncan. "Knowledge and Final Value." In *The Nature and Value of Knowledge: Three Investigations*, by Duncan Pritchard, Alan Millar, and Adrian Haddock. Oxford: Oxford University Press, 2010.

"Quick Facts." United States Census Bureau. Accessed November 20, 2023. https://www.census.gov/quickfacts/fact/table/US/PST045222.

Ramirez, Clifford A. *FERPA Clear and Simple: The College Professional's Guide to Compliance*. New York: John Wiley and Sons, 2009.

Reed, Stephen. *Entrepreneurship Law: Cases and Materials*. New York: Wolters Kluwer Law and Business, 2013.

Regis, Edward. "What Is Ethical Egoism?" *Ethics* 91, no. 1 (1980): 50–62.

Reinhardt, Tobias. Introduction to *Dialogues and Essays*, by Lucius Annaeus Seneca. Translated by John Davie. New York: Oxford University Press, 2007.

Robinson, David T., and Berk A. Sensoy. "Cyclicality, Performance Measurement, and Cash Flow Liquidity in Private Equity." *Journal of Financial Economics* 122, no. 3 (2016): 521–543.

Rodríguez, José E., Kendall M. Campbell, and Linda H. Pololi. "Addressing Disparities in Academic Medicine: What of the Minority Tax?" *BMC Medical Education* 15, no. 1 (2015): 1–5.

Rosen, Sherwin. "The Economics of Superstars." *American Economic Review* 71, no. 5 (1981): 845–858.

Rubin, Aaron. "Implementing and Enforcing Online Terms of Use: Socially Aware." *JD supra*, 2014. https://www.jdsupra.com/legalnews/implementing-and-enforcing-online-terms-94832.

Ruef, Martin. "Entrepreneurial Groups." In *Historical Foundations of Entrepreneurship Research*, edited by Hans Landström and Franz Lohrke. Cheltenham, UK: Edward Elgar Publishing, 2010.

Ryle, Gilbert. "Knowing How and Knowing That: The Presidential Address." *Proceedings of the Aristotelian Society* 46 (1945): 1–16.

Samila, Sampsa, and Olav Sorenson. "Community and Capital in Entrepreneurship and Economic Growth." *American Sociological Review* 82, no. 4 (2017): 770–795.

Sanchez-Burks, Jeffrey, David J. Brophy, Thomas Jensen, Melanie Milovac, and Evgeny Kagan. "Mentoring in Startup Ecosystems." Ross School of Business Paper No. 1376. 2017. https://papers.ssrn.com/sol3/papers.cfm?abstract_id=3066168.

Schoemaker, Paul J. H. "The Future Challenges of Business: Rethinking Management Education." *California Management Review* 50, no. 3 (2008): 119–139.

Schrage, Michael. *The Innovator's Hypothesis: How Cheap Experiments Are Worth More Than Good Ideas*. Cambridge, MA: MIT Press, 2016.

Schumpeter, Joseph A. *Capitalism, Socialism, and Democracy*. New York: Harper and Brothers, 1942.

Schumpeter, Joseph A. *The Theory of Economic Development*. Cambridge, MA: Harvard University Press, 1934.

Schuwerk, Robert P. "The Law Professor as Fiduciary: What Duties Do We Owe to Our Students." *South Texas Law Review* 45 (Fall 2004): 753–812.

Shane, Scott. "Why Hiring Non-Academics to Teach Entrepreneurship Is a Bad Idea." *Small Business Trends*, October 3, 2016.

Shane, Scott, and Sankaran Venkataraman. "The Promise of Entrepreneurship as a Field." *Academy of Management Review* 25, no. 1 (2000): 217–226.

Sidgwick, Henry. *The Methods of Ethics*. London: Palgrave Macmillan, 1962.

Siegel, Robin, Eric Siegel, and Ian C. Macmillan. "Characteristics Distinguishing High-Growth Ventures." *Journal of Business Venturing* 8, no. 2 (1993): 169–180.

Silvernagel, Craig A., Myrna R. Olson, and Robert H. Stupnisky. "Mine, Yours, or Ours? Perceptions of Student-Created Intellectual Property Ownership." *Entrepreneurship Education and Pedagogy* 4, no. 3 (2021): 204–224.

Small, Will. "The Transmission of Skill." *Philosophical Topics* 42, no. 1 (2014): 85–111.

Smallwood, Mary Lovett. *An Historical Study of Examinations and Grading Systems in Early American Universities: A Critical Study of the Original Records of Harvard, William and Mary, Yale, Mount Holyoke, and Michigan from Their Founding to 1900*. Cambridge, MA: Harvard University Press, 1935.

Smith, Adam. *The Theory of Moral Sentiments: To Which Is Added, a Dissertation on the Origin of Languages*. Dublin: J. Beatty and C. Jackson, 1777. https://www.gutenberg.org/cache/epub/67363/pg67363-images.html.

Smith, Cedric M. "Origin and Uses of *Primum Non Nocere*—Above All, Do No Harm!" *Journal of Clinical Pharmacology* 45, no. 4 (2005): 371–377.

"Starting a Business as a Student." Business.gov.nl. Accessed November 21, 2023. https://business.gov.nl/starting-your-business/various-starting-points/starting-a -business-as-a-student.

"Starting a Business in Germany with a Student Visa?" Bundesministerium für Wirtschaft und Klimaschutz. Accessed November 21, 2023. https://www.existenzgrue nder.de/SharedDocs/BMWi-Expertenforum/English-Version/Starting-a-Business-in -Germany-with-a-Student-Visa.html.

Steinbauer, Robert, Nicholas D. Rhew, Eric Kinnamon, and Frances Fabian. "The Conflicting Drivers of Entrepreneurial Ethics." *Journal of Ethics and Entrepreneurship* 4, no. 1 (2014): 57–72.

Steiner, Susanne. "Not Just the What and How, but Also the Who: The Impact of Entrepreneurship Educators." In *Handbook on the Entrepreneurial University*, edited by Alain Fayolle and Dana T. Redford. Cheltenham, UK: Edward Elgar Publishing, 2014.

Steup, Matthias. "Epistemology." In *The Stanford Encyclopedia of Philosophy*, edited by Edward N. Zalta. Summer 2018. https://plato.stanford.edu/archives/sum2018 /entries/epistemology.

Sullivan, Roger. *An Introduction to Kant's Ethics*. New York: Cambridge University Press, 1994.

Sun, Jasmine, Theresa Gao, Sasha Perigo, Shanta Katipamula, Kimiko Hirota, Maia Brockbank, and Emma Tsurkov. "Stanford Doesn't Trust Joe Lonsdale to Mentor Students; You Shouldn't Either." *Stanford Daily*, March 15, 2019.

Swanton, Christine. "Virtue Ethics, Role Ethics, and Business Ethics." In *Working Virtue: Virtue Ethics and Contemporary Moral Problems*, edited by Rebecca L. Walker and Philip J. Ivanhoe. Oxford: Clarendon Press, 2007.

Thompson, Nicholas. "The End of Stanford?" *New Yorker*, April 8, 2013.

Thompson, Nicholas. "Stanford and Its Startups." *New Yorker*, September 11, 2013.

Thomson, Judith Jarvis. "The Trolley Problem." *Yale Law Journal* 94, no. 6 (1985): 1395–1415.

Tolentino, Jia. "The Promise of Vaping and the Rise of JUUL." *New Yorker*, May 14, 2018.

Torrance, Wendy E. F. "Entrepreneurial Campuses: Action, Impact, and Lessons Learned from the Kauffman Campuses Initiative." Ewing Marion Kauffman Foundation, 2013. https://www.kauffman.org/wp-content/uploads/2019/12/entrepreneurial campusesessay.pdf.

Van Der Sluis, Justin, Mirjam Van Praag, and Wim Vijverberg. "Education and Entrepreneurship Selection and Performance: A Review of the Empirical Literature." *Journal of Economic Surveys* 22, no. 5 (2008): 795–841.

Van Praag, Mirjam, and Peter H. Versloot. 2007. "The Economic Benefits and Costs of Entrepreneurship: A Review of the Research." *Foundations and Trends in Entrepreneurship* 4, no. 2 (2007): 65–154.

Van Praag, Mirjam, Arjen van Witteloostuijn, and Justin Van Der Sluis. "The Higher Returns to Formal Education for Entrepreneurs versus Employees." *Small Business Economics* 40 (2013): 375–396.

Veysey, Laurence R. *The Emergence of the American University.* Chicago: University of Chicago Press, 1970.

Walsh, Grace S., and James A. Cunningham. "Business Failure and Entrepreneurship: Emergence, Evolution and Future Research." *Foundations and Trends in Entrepreneurship* 12, no. 3 (2016): 163–285.

Wasserman, Noam. *The Founder's Dilemmas: Anticipating and Avoiding the Pitfalls That Can Sink a Startup.* Princeton, NJ: Princeton University Press, 2013.

Weeks, Kent, and Rich Haglund. "Fiduciary Duties of College and University Faculty and Administrators." *Journal of College and University Law* 29, no. 1 (2002): 153–187.

Weis, Gregory F. "Grading." *Teaching Philosophy* 18, no. 1 (1995): 3–13.

Williams, Bernard. *Moral Luck: Philosophical Papers 1973–1980.* New York: Cambridge University Press, 1981.

Williamson, Timothy, and Jason Stanley. "Knowing How." *Journal of Philosophy* 98, no. 8 (2001): 411–444.

Winthrop, John. "A Model of Christian Charity." Teaching American History. Accessed November 21, 2023. https://teachingamericanhistory.org/document/a-model-of-christian-charity-2.

Wright, Sarah L., and Jerome A. Katz. "Protecting Student Intellectual Property in the Entrepreneurial Classroom." *Journal of Management Education* 40, no. 2 (2016): 152–169.

Yale College, Committee of the Corporation, and the Academical Faculty. "Report of the Faculty." New Haven, CT: Hezekiah Howe, 1828. http://www.keithbuhler.com/content/ebooks/yalereport.pdf.

Index